MOTEL
AMERICA

MOTEL AMERICA

A STATE-BY-STATE TOUR GUIDE TO NOSTALGIC STOPOVERS

Andrew F. Wood

Jenny L. Wood

COLLECTOR'S PRESS

PORTLAND, OREGON

Design: Wade Daughtry, Collectors Press, Inc.
Editor: Aimee Stoddard

Printed in China
First American edition
9 8 7 6 5 4 3 2 1

Collectors Press books are available at special discounts for bulk purchases, premiums, and promotions. Special editions, including personalized inserts or covers, and corporate logos, can be printed in quantity for special purposes. For further information contact: Special Sales, Collectors Press, Inc., PO Box 230986, Portland, OR 97281. Toll free: 1-800-423-1848.

For a free catalog write: Collectors Press, Inc., PO Box 230986, Portland, OR 97281.
Toll free: 1-800-423-1848 or visit our website at: collectorspress.com.

Jenny and I appreciate the support we received from San Jose State University and Seagate Technology as we've taken countless days off to travel the country and write this book. We are doubly grateful for the many local historians, dedicated preservation societies, and visitors to our Motel Americana website who offered advice and (mostly) accurate directions to guide our path.

We share our respect and admiration for the hundreds of Mom and Pop motel owners, groggy night clerks, and bemused residents (both short- and long-term) who greeted our visits with patience and good humor. And we share our appreciation for dozens of friends and family who helped us keep the home fires warm without burning down the house.

Finally, we express love for our daughter, Vienna, who has tolerated this strange obsession over the years as we showed her a country marked by its small places. We hope that her generation will continue to celebrate the neon buzz of the open road and remember to "look for America" beyond the superslab. It's still there.

— Andrew F. Wood & Jenny L. Wood

INTRODUCTION

The vast interstate stretches on for miles. Wheezy RVs covered with stickers from every tourist trap that ever sold a backscratcher compete with darting sports cars whose drivers pound their dashboards in frustration. Government issued road signs offer little respite from the crushing monotony of the traffic jam. Occasionally, a rebellious motorist maneuvers into the emergency lane, then takes the exit ramp to oblivion. The sign reads "Services," meaning that predictable theme restaurants, chain hotels, and droning strip malls are not far. Without thinking, you turn the wheel and lay on the gas. Your former world, the traffic jam of angry, depressed, sullen strangers, goes on for miles and miles. Now, you're in the middle of nowhere and there's no speed limit posted.

Hours pass as you careen 'round hills and alongside pastures. Every twenty minutes or so you catch the telltale signs of a town: an old cemetery, some rusting farm equipment for sale, a few hand-painted posters advertising an ice cream social held two months ago. You slow down even though you know the cops are sleeping by now. You're searching for a Mom and Pop motel, not a Bed and Breakfast, not a downtown hotel with fancy lobby and pricey room. Up ahead you envision a tacky neon sign glowing. Perhaps some of the wiring has rusted and the letters don't all work. Maybe it's a giant cactus, metal boll weevil, or an ethereal red and yellow sunset. Or perhaps you'll find a time capsule of yesterday's tomorrows: a neon rocket, a glowing sputnik, a jaunty atomic glyph. Of course, you find more than mere history. You find a culture of mobility.

Motels reflect a particular component of a fascinating evolution of roadside lodging. At the turn of the twentieth century, you would find few of the amenities available to today's interstate traveler. In his outstanding history of the evolution of motels from autocamps, *Americans on the Road*, Warren James Belasco describes how folks traveling west of the Mississippi found camping to be a perfect alternative to expensive hotels. Indeed, the convenience and anonymity of a farmer's field or lakeshore was plenty inviting.

In her book, *A Long Way from Boston*, Beth O'Shea recalls her visit to one of these camps:

> *"Is this a tourist camp?" I asked, looking around with interest. We had heard about them, but had expected something more elaborate.*
>
> *"Sure, it's a tourist camp," he told us. "Anythin's a tourist camp what has*

water and no no-trespass signs. All the towns has got 'em now. They figure they give you a place where you can pitch your tent and you'll buy food and stuff at their stores."

At first, towns and villages welcomed auto tourists and their vacation cash. However, it didn't take long for locals to complain about the mess, the commotion, and even the loose morals of auto gypsies. They were often labeled Tin Can Tourists who traveled "with one shirt and a $20 bill — and they didn't change either."

As the Depression wore on, it became profitable to offer more amenities than were available at the campsite. Farmers and other business folk would contract with an oil company, put up a gas pump, and throw up a few shacks. Some were pre-fab; others were handmade. In their comprehensive book *The Motel in America*, John Jakle, Keith Sculle, and Jefferson Rogers illustrate the typical visit:

> *At the U-Smile Cabin Camp . . . arriving guests signed the registry and then paid their money. A cabin without a mattress rented for one dollar; a mattress for two people cost an extra twenty-five cents, and blankets,*

sheets, and pillows another fifty cents. The manager rode the running boards to show guests to their cabins. Each guest was given a bucket of water from an outside hydrant, along with a scuttle of firewood in the winter.

Cottage courts (also known as tourist courts) emerged to add some class to these otherwise dingy collections. They were standardized along a common motif and frequently organized around a public lawn. However, the manager's office and sign began to take more ostentatious forms. Unlike downtown hotels, courts were designed to be auto-mobile friendly. You could park next to your individual room or even in your own garage.

Along with filling stations, cafes began to appear at these roadside havens. The Sanders Court advertised "complete accommodations with tile baths (abundance of hot water), carpeted floors, 'Perfect Sleeper' beds, air conditioned, steam heated, radio in every room, open all year, serving excellent food." Today, you can visit the KFC in Corbin on the site where the Harland Sanders phenomenon began.

World War II brought a rationing of everything related to tourism. Tires, gasoline, and most of all, leisure time were at a premium. However, as troops crossed the country on orders to head overseas, they caught visions of America and planned to see it again with their families. At night, they found motor courts — no longer isolated cottages, but fully integrated buildings under a single roof — lit by neon, designed with flair, and eventually referred to as "motels." While the rooms were plain and functional, the facades took advantage of regional styles (and, occasionally, stereotypes). Owners employed stucco, adobe, stone, brick — whatever was handy — to attract guests.

Many motel owners settled in for a life's work. However, those plans were demolished as interstates began to snake across the nation in the 1950s and 1960s. Before long, small-time motor courts were rendered obsolete by chains that began to blur the distinction between motels and hotels. Single story structures gave way to double and triple deckers. The thrill of discovering the unique look and feel of a roadside motel was replaced by assurances of sameness "from coast to coast."

Nowadays, few people go out of their way to find roadside motels. Fewer still remember the traditions of autocamps and tourist courts. However, a growing number of preservation societies and intrepid cultural explorers have begun to hit the exits and travel the highways again in search of that one singular experience just around the bend.

This book represents our effort to celebrate the Mom and Pop motels that have managed to endure decades of social upheaval, changing tastes, bypassed highways, and declining fortunes in towns across the nation. We have crossed the country on multiple trips, searching for roads that William Least Heat Moon famously popularized as "blue highways." We have interviewed hundreds of motel owners and guests and collected thousands of postcards, ashtrays, matchbook covers, and car decals. Like its predecessor from Collectors Press, *Road Trip America: A State-By-State Tour Guide to Offbeat Destinations*, this book is organized by state, not by chronology or style. We've striven to offer a balanced account through photographs, narratives, anecdotes, and artifacts of the special character of these places — as well as the places where you can meet some special characters. Occasionally, history and sentiment have demanded that we mention relics and ruins whose power to draw us off the road continues after the motel lost its battle with the bulldozer.

In our effort to catalog some of our most beloved motels in each of the fifty states, we make no promise that we've visited every motel in the nation. We simply offer a sample of the weird, wild, and wonderful motor courts that we've encountered during eight years of research. As you plan your journey, use our book as a guide but not as a replacement for the serendipity that follows a chance conversation with folks you meet on your *own* search.

After all, the search of a great motel is more than a quest for a comfortable bed and quiet night followed by an anonymous departure the next morning. When you find a motel with that certain neon sign or an aging tourist court where strangers rest on metal chairs and share advice, you've found a treasure. Find it by accident. Stay for the sheer pleasure of it. And come back soon.

ALABAMA

Alabama, known as the "Heart of Dixie," has become an uneasy gathering place for immigrants from around the world who have chosen to run motels in small towns across the state. Occasionally, they encounter the rough edge of Alabama's historically troubled relationship with outsiders but, for the most part, the newcomers have found themselves welcome and have chosen to make their new homes in communities in which "y'all aren't from around here are you" could easily be their motto. Near the Georgia border in Phenix City (spelled that way to differentiate the city from the Arizona version), Kailas Desai has just added new rooms and works to refurbish her office. In Greenville, along Highway 31, Dahya Patel has painted the logo for his "Reid Motel" in bright reds and yellows on the satellite dish. Both, strangers to each other, reflect a common feature in the changing face of American motel ownership: the value of these Mom

and Pop establishments in anchoring new families into the fabric of American life.

Visiting with them, and with the thousands of old timers who continue to run their own tiny motels, requires a departure from high-speed travel. For example, when passing over the swampy expanse between Alabama and Louisiana, you might be inspired to take Interstate 10 with its zippy speed limits and limited obstructions, but you'll miss out on a glorious mini-mecca of neon at the western edge of Mobile. Starting with the Beverly Motel, you'll swoon at the sight of a neon figure based on Jantzen's immortal "diving girl," once one of the most recognized logos in the world. Caught in a graceful leap, her body arching toward imaginary water below, Beverly advertises one of the few small motels that offer swimming pools any-

more. Continuing down the road, you'll see another glowing beauty. The Olsson Motel greets you with red neon strips and a pulsating star, proving that the folks in Mobile dig the electronic nightlife. Plenty of other examples wait in town, most notably the Bama Motel with a funky pitched roof in the googie style, offering evidence of Mobile's appreciation of its roadside past.

While in Mobile, you might also engage in a bit of time travel along Highway 90, searching for remains of the St. Francis Hotel Courts, eventually renamed the St. Francis Motor Hotel. The St. Francis was part of the Alamo Plaza chain of motor inns, each of which greeted visitors with a pueblo revival facade that suggested memories of the Texas fort that burned itself into American history with the aid of John Wayne films. By the 1960s, the mythic power of Alamo imagery had played itself out in Mobile and the facade was replaced with a more staid brick wall broken by ornamental panels that gave the appearance of a mausoleum for roadside travelers. Chatting with a docent at the Historic Mobile Preservation Society, his drawl dripping with southern syrup, you'll find that the motel was abandoned and destroyed almost twenty years ago to make way for a shopping center. Today, the former link in the Alamo chain resides only in postcards and the tricks of memory.

ALASKA

To put it delicately, motels in **Alaska** tend to be plain, understated, and even boring. Of course, when visiting the "Last Frontier," you might forgive motel owners for thinking that you'll save your photographing talents for the state's glaciers, fjords, and majestic peaks. After all, how

The nearly florescent quality of green walls and yellow gables barely overcome the homespun simplicity of a hand-painted sign: "Enjoy Nice Modern Motel." If you restrict your search for beauty to the human-made environment, you're looking in the wrong state.

can a small line of motel rooms (with requisite coffee makers and queen sized beds) compete with a panoramic view split by vast fields and towering mountains? Moreover, when visiting a land of snow and ice, you can rest assured that anyone who works with neon does so out of whimsy and a bit of madness; thus the signs are wooden and nearly invisible at night. One regional photographer, Henk Binnendijk, captures the mood perfectly with his photo of a Ninilchik Beach Motel.

Traveling to Alaska (just try to keep that Johnny Horton song "North to Alaska" out of your mind), you'll want to journey up the Alaska Highway, a drive labeled by some commentators as the country's best road trip. Soon after departing the Canadian Yukon, set your course for Tok (rhymes with Poke), a town named after a mascot puppy beloved by the engineers who helped build the wartime road through this area. The local Tok Lodge has served as home to Pam and Buddy Johnson

for nearly three decades. It's the "kind of place they like to stay when they travel." But call ahead; its prime location as a jumping off point is already well known.

Head west to Seward, so named for the cabinet secretary whose idea to purchase the Alaska territory from the Russians earned the state its unofficial nickname of "Seward's Folly." Located near the Kenai Fjords and known for offering views of whales in the Gulf of Alaska, Seward also offers a nice accommodation in Murphy's Motel. Built in 1953, the motel withstood an earthquake nine years later that folks still discuss with awed tones. Today, visitors can check out the Halibut Derby, a Polar Bear "Jump Off," and even a Seward Jazz Festival.

If you plan to journey north to Fairbanks, make sure you stop by the Golden North Motel. Paul and Betty Baer know the Last Frontier intimately. Betty remembers when Alaska was admitted as a state, and Paul arrived in 1960 during his time with the Army. Maintaining their humble two-story, low-rise motel offers the Baers an opportunity to dispense advice about dog sledding, ice sculpture, and gold mining. Of course, one unforgettable experience awaits golfers. The Fairbanks North Star Golf Club allows you to play under the midnight sun in North America's northern-most golf course. Watch out for roaming moose and remember the course rule: "When a raven or fox steals a golf ball, a replacement may be dropped without penalty at the scene of the crime."

ARIZONA

For many visitors to **Arizona**, their first view of the Grand Canyon State is overhead as they fly into the Phoenix metropolis. From the plane, they see firsthand the impact of cheap land and a booming population. Asphalt sprawls for miles and miles in every direction into the desert, leaving golf courses and video stores in its wake. Driving the interstate, you can pass

exits like ticks of a clock, each the same as before. Take the Mesa exit and you'll discover a surprise next to the faded green shuffleboard court and soupy pool of the tired Starlight Motel: a fantasy of pink and purple as a buxom bathing beauty dives

repeatedly into a glistening, electronic splash. For years, photographers have experimented with their exposure settings in a quest to capture each of the three animated steps of the diving girl plummeting into the pool.

To the north, Route 66 threads its way through mesas and vast stretches of open land where the cities have not yet taken root. In Kingman, bikers with bandanas over their faces pull off to grab a soda and peer down the highway. At the Siesta Motel, sheets hanging from a clothesline billow in the warm breeze. Aligning the rooms, refrigerator-sized air conditioning units hang from metal rods, their filters transformed into piles of rusted spaghetti-wire. The owner comes out and we chat a bit. Though she's run the Siesta for nineteen years, a Brooklyn-esque dialect manages to add some toughness to her prose. But when one of the locals, a San Diego refugee wearing denim and a craggy grin, complains about how hard it is to walk to the local grocery store, she smiles broadly and teases: "Oh, you know I'd drive you."

If you cruise the Mother Road back to Holbrook, don't forget to pay your respects at the Wigwam Village. Part of a tiny chain of teepee motels launched by Frank A. Redford, the Village reflects an age in American roadside design marked by

SKY RIDERS HOTEL — PHOENIX, ARIZONA

mimetic architecture, buildings that look like the things they advertise. So if you're going to eat in a Mexican restaurant shaped like a giant sombrero or going to grab a cup of Joe in a diner shaped like a coffee pot, why not sleep in a motel shaped like a teepee? The Arizona version emerged from a deal between Redford and Chester Lewis. Redford would hand over the blueprints for the unique ten-sided buildings (complete with private bathrooms) for a percentage of dimes collected by the pay-to-play radios installed in each teepee. And, apparently, neither would kid the other about the embarrassing fact that teepees are not wigwams. Decades later, the Holbrook Wigwam Village endures as one of three remaining teepee motels inspired by Redford's plans.

For Arizona's funkiest vibe, head all the way south to Tucson, a town whose gorgeous neon signs and motel relics are almost perfectly photographed in Abigail Gumbiner and Carol Hayden's book, *Vacant Eden*. Try not to get run over as you photograph the Tucson Inn with its poles bursting skyward like sunrays. Make sure you seek out the Arizona Motel whose pink and green neon casts an otherworldly glow when the sun sets. And shuffle quietly past the literally named No-Tel Motel, while trying to contain your snigger. Or, you can loosen your hair for a high-speed

burn to Yuma in search of the Yuma Cabana Motel, scorching near the Mexico border. You'll put down a few more bills, but the rooms are cleaner. The sign boasts, it's "out of this world," a phrase that evokes nostalgia for the 1960s. Laugh now, but when you see it, you'll understand.

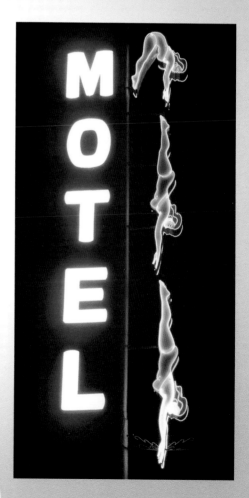

ARKANSAS

While visiting **Arkansas**, you should plan to slow down in Hot Springs, noted for its ornate bathhouses where turn-of-the-century tourists would "take the waters." Sadly, many of the tourist courts on either side of the city center suffer the ravages of prostitution and drug use. For a lover of genuine Mom and Pop stops, there are sev-

A no-nonsense guy, Efren rents and cleans every room himself: "I don't trust anyone else to do it — not even my wife." He's proud of a recent accolade his Cottage Motel received from a local booster club as the town's most beautiful small business, but often regrets his decision to flee the hassles and traffic of New York. The prom-

PARKWAY COURT, 815 Park Ave, Hot Springs National Park, Ark.

eral nice choices though. You might enjoy the Victorian embellishments that set the Tower Motel apart from most cookie-cutter chains, or you could seek out the Fountain Motel that reflects a glorious vision of streamline-moderne design. But, you should end your tour with the Cottage Motel on Park Avenue. While insects begin to practice their musical cacophony under a setting sun, pull into the court and meet Efren. Remember: he's not only the owner, he's also the "president."

ise of loose gamblers visiting casinos in Hot Springs never panned out thanks to local bible thumpers. Despite the potential for a quick profit, he won't sell his motel cheap: "I'm not going to give it away. I spent a lot of money renovating this place. I sweated my blood here."

To the northwest in Eureka Springs, the Tall Pines Motor Inn has welcomed guests seeking refuge from the hustle of the highway since Phillip and Alice Nordquest moved from Chicago and built the rustic

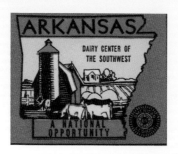

cabins in 1947. Listed on the National Register of Historic Places, the Tall Pines Motor Inn manages to exude a secluded feel despite its proximity to a regional tourist center. For travelers seeking the kind of authenticity that comes with sites placed on the National Register, you might as well return to Hot Springs in search of the Green Elf Court. Now idling away as an apartment complex, the Green Elf gained its named through a contest whose winner, Kittie Thornton, inspired the notion of a tourist court as a "Fairyland of Comfort." Today, the site offers a significant example of Craftsman "Airplane Bungalow" design, the kind in which the extended roofline resembles the wings of a flying machine.

Jill Corran, a Little Rock expert on motel preservation who shared much of the historical background about Arkansas motels for the writing of this section, tells us the most clever naming story may be found in the south-central Arkansas town of Fordyce. There, along Highway 167, a fellow named Deen (his spelling, yes) Kilgore went broke giving out too much credit in his grocery store. Vowing never to make the same mistake again, he opened a motel and restaurant that provided an essential stop for traveling salesmen until the 1970s. Of course, you don't offer "panelray heat" and telephones in each room on credit. Thus the name of his motel, BOCO Courts, stood for "Bought on Cash Only."

BIL-ROY HOTEL AND SERVICE STATION, West Memphis, Ark.

CALIFORNIA

The **California** heat shimmers off the asphalt as the road slides past the scorching town of Blythe, making an ascent to bounteous lands and blue harbors. At the Sea Shell Motel, Johnston and his wife have stretched their social security checks to maintain a tenuous hold on the motel. Sitting under one of several dozen condemnation notices, both despair at the motel's shabby condition. If the previous owner, a woman they call Grandma, were still alive, "she'd turn over in her grave."

Better head northwest toward Barstow where the Route 66 Motel tells a happier story. Built in 1922, the motel offers an example to other towns seeking to revitalize their aging main street districts that might otherwise decay. Ved and Mridu Shandil have refurbished the formerly nondescript motel into a Mother Road must-see complete with antique cars between the cottages and round beds in many of the rooms. The couple shows visitors a guest book filled with the names and memories of road-trippers from around the world, many of whom have left photos and other memorabilia. For Ved and Mridu, the Route 66 Motel is more than a business, it's their passion: "Number one: this is Americana. Number two: We are proud to be in Barstow."

Further West in Mojave, Bill White celebrates the legacy of his grandmother, N.E. Mobley, a woman who dared to enter business school and run a motel in an era when the word "proprietress" still earned clucks from the city fathers. As the vast aqueducts began snaking their way through the desert landscape of yuccas and Joshua trees, she built a garage and cafe, raised a family, and inspired her grandson to stay in the business. Today, White's Motel offers a kidney-shaped pool, the smell of roses and violets, and a chance to pet the mammoth family poodle.

In Rialto, the motel room teepees of the Wigwam Village continue their resurgence after years of neglect. The slogan still reads, "Do it in a Teepee," yet numerous signs warn guests that they reside under constant videotaped surveillance. The pool is filled with a murky substance, the consistency of pancake syrup. But the teepees have been

recently painted and the lawn has been freshly mowed. The Rialto Wigwam Village is on its way back from the brink.

Head north along 99 and you'll find the ruins and relics that inspired glorious linen postcards, color-saturated images that never quite reflected the more mundane motels they advertised. Head toward the coast, and pay homage to the site of the world's first motel about a mile north of San Luis Obispo on 101. In 1925, Arthur Heinman invested about $80,000 into the Milestone Motel — eventually renamed the Motel Inn. Built in Spanish revival, the Motel Inn invites highway aficionados to visit a vision of crass commercialism,

derivative architecture, and bypassed dreams. There are so few genuine "firsts" anymore- but the Motel Inn is indeed the first motel: It's a quick stop along the highway designed to eschew the ponderous ritual of hotel lobby check-in and management surveillance. Thanks to this architectural innovation, highway voyagers could imagine themselves as upscale hobos, cruising along the winding road, stopping for a while to await the dew of the next morning, then heading again toward the horizon. The Motel Inn awaits contractors and preservationists who discuss restoration. But no one is sure when that day will come.

COLORADO

Members United
Motor Courts, Inc.
AAA

U. S. Highway No. 85 and 87
1700 South Santa Fe
DENVER, COLORADO

While **Colorado** offers a panorama of stunning mountain views and an impressive array of hiking and camping opportunities, one of its most unique novelties may be found in the peculiar combination of motel and movie theater. The Movie Manner Motor Inn in Monte Vista offers two stories of rooms facing an outdoor screen, allowing you to park your car before twilight, grab some popcorn from the concession stand, fluff up the pillows on your bed, and watch a first-run film from your very own room. A rare experience (comparable only to the Fairlee Movie Motel in Vermont), the Movie Manner illustrates a perfect balance of America's love of travel and need for home.

More traditional accommodations may be found at the Siesta Motel in Durango whose southwestern style accomplishes the goal of all vernacular architecture: it serves to remind you that you're not from around here. For uptight urban dwellers, the entire town evokes a sense of place that cannot be reproduced easily. Once labeled the "worst-dressed town in America" (by no less qualified fashion mavens than the pithy commentators of *USA Today*), Durango seems to come by its "ah shucks" response to the constant trickle of bemused tourists genuinely. Once you kick off your spurs at the Siesta, you might amble downtown on a clear summer evening and catch the show at the Bar D Chuckwagon where (if you're very lucky), you can chuckle at the world-renowned "commode-a-phone."

Entering Colorado from the East? You might as well check out Pueblo and some of the most annoying vehicular pacification systems (also known as speed bumps) known to humankind. But don't stop long or you'll be disappointed. Head north on Interstate 25 (gritting your teeth through traffic, construction, and the indignity of superslab travel) and you'll find one of the most awesome displays of mid-century

motel design in the nation. Ranking easily with Tucumcari, New Mexico, and Wildwood, New Jersey, the towns of Colorado Springs and Manitou Springs offer a stunning collection of animated signage and glowing neon. Included in this gorgeous assemblage is the La Fon with a sign that would break the ordinances of ninety-nine percent of American cities for height and brightness. Across the street, you can grab a turkey sandwich at Moe's Diner that rivals anything you might get at a big city diner. The conversation with local folks comes free with the meal. Staying the night? Head back to Colorado Springs and the Chief Motel where a neon warrior invites you — tomahawk in hand — off the road for a snooze. The motel offers a great value as well as an unforgettable combination of tackiness and charm. Eventually, you'll be drawn to Denver, confident that a city with such a vast main street (Colfax Avenue stretches 26 miles) ought to boast a fair number of motels. Sure enough, the green-cactus-shaped A Bar D Motel, the Big Bunny Motel (once called "Bugs Bunny" before some nasty legal intervention), and the Rocky Mtn. Motel with its weatherworn mountainous peaks represent a photographer's dream. But you'll want to keep driving through town. On the east end of Colfax, you'll find the Top Star Motel, at home in an area in which virtually every sign warns against the scourges of crime, drug use, and unregistered guests. Indeed, as you contemplate your accommodations along the main Denver thoroughfare, remember this piece of advice: a motel that offers "sleeping rooms" probably doesn't provide a continental breakfast.

MOUNTAIN VIEW COURTS
FINEST CAMP at COLORADO SPRINGS, COLO. South Edge of Town
Highway U. S. 85 — Steam Heat — B. C. White, Prop.

Connecticut challenges lovers of tacky Mom and Pop motels who seek garish neon and vernacular signs. Who would have imagined glowing cacti, concrete teepees, or googie sputniks in The Constitution State? Indeed, the northeastern portion of Connecticut maintains the quaint moniker of "The Quiet Corner" due to its lack of tacky architecture and electronic nightlife. Writing in the *New York Times*, Erik Sandberg-Diment notes that when photographed from space, the Corner provides the only "black hole in the illumination of the earth between Washington and Boston." This "Last Green Valley" seems built precisely for day-tripping antiquers who might pause for tea at a tourist home and stay over on their next anniversary. Seekers of buzzing signs might as well keep on driving.

Along the state's southern coast, towns dart in out of view, hidden by tree-lined curves and green fields. Dip near the water and you'll find the town of Mystic. Yes, the one in the pizza movie that launched a thousand smiles from Julia Roberts. Trudging through the weekend traffic comprised of mammoth SUVs, you'll find solace at the Old Mystic Motor Lodge, a pleasant alternative to the endless hive of faceless chains and pricey B&Bs. Built in the late 1960s, the motel offers the institutional look and feel of a mid-century high school, safe but

forgettable. Nonetheless, the folks there seem genuinely happy to offer advice on local attractions.

Heading toward New Haven, slow down in Westbrook and gawk at the single, tiny white cabins of the appropriately named Cabins Motel. Reminiscent of an age before the emergence of I-shaped and L-shaped motels, the Cabins offer a tiny private ownership fantasy: a room of your own for a few dollars. But if you're planning to stay for a week on the Connecticut shore, there's really only one choice: A Victorian Village Inn on Route 1 near Clinton. There, Patrice LePera and her

husband Al Lynch have refitted a bunch of formerly dilapidated cabins into a Gingerbread fantasy of roses, birdhouses, and fancy latticework. Lit by gas lamps and filled with antiques, the Village offers a unique time travel experience for lovers of nineteenth century art and design.

Before leaving Connecticut, drop by Yale University Art Gallery in West Haven. If you're lucky, you'll find displayed a most vivid and poignant roadside image: Edward Hopper's 1957 "Western Motel." A subdued pallet of somber greens, hazy mauves, and ominous blues, "Motel" reenacts Hopper's penchant for displaying people who appear to occupy places without actually living within them. In the painting, a lone woman sits in a chair next to a zipped bag; outside, a car awaits. Staring back at us through the frame, she dares us to imagine where she's going and how long she's been away from home. Like Hopper's "Nighthawk's Cafe" and "Gas," "Western Motel" presents modern life as a series of lonely tableaus where desperate loners lose themselves in thought and solitude. Rather than view the image in this book, its power sapped through mechanical reproduction, you might as well get in your car and see it for yourself.

DELAWARE

Calling itself "the First State," **Delaware** does not necessarily come first in motel attractions. If you seek sparkling sun and sand, stick with the coastline from Lewes down to Fenwick Island. There, languid tourists soak up the rays and seek out the boardwalks for hot dogs and cotton candy. When cruising the coast, you'll probably want to focus your attention to Rehoboth Beach where you'll have little difficulty finding a nice motel near the surf. However, most offer typical accommodations — some beach chairs, a few tiki torches, and high summer rates. It's a sad fact mirrored up and down both coasts that motels that catch your eye without emptying your wallet are hard to come by.

Even so, the Anchorage Motel offers one of the better spots you'll find in the area. It's family owned and the rates are reasonable.

Cruising away from the coast to catch U.S. 13 back north toward Wilmington and the Philadelphia grid beyond presents some pretty countryside, but few decent motels. The Pleasant Hill Motel has stood for decades but has fallen on hard times recently. Only when you intersect with the National Road, known these days as Highway 40, will you encounter a scraggle of motels you won't soon forget. Here, you remember that many former Mom and Pop motels have become homes to down-and-out travelers who work when they can and move on when they must. The town of Bear presents a good picture of motel life for these folks. There, at the West Motel, a sad assortment of locals and transients pass the days chatting, partying, and worrying about when the next cold gust will knock them back on the highway.

DELAWARE

Down the road, you'll find an ancient motel whose name is obscured by trees. The office sign reads, "Beware of dog. Don't trust the cat either." Sure enough, a yip of dachshunds announce your presence. Another decimated reminder of happier days long gone? Perhaps. But as the manager takes you from room to room, introducing you to friendly folks who have made this motel their home, you encounter a different vibe than any other motel along this decaying stretch of road. The owners here have decided to turn their motel around, to refurbish the rooms and bring the place back from the brink. The only thing they need is a name you can read from the road.

Perhaps the most well-known motel where Highways 40 and 13 meet remains the Hollywood Motel. An old postcard reads, "All rooms luxuriously furnished in the most modern furniture, Beautyrest mattresses." Today, the U-shaped structure casts a modern appearance with its block glass and tan brick facade. Best of all, the motel features not one but two stunning signs that will tickle any roadside photographer's fancy. The Hollywood Motel, though, resides in that nether region between roadside oasis and temporary exile. No one quite knows which way the story will end for this one.

Park Plaza Motel
U.S. Route 13 & 40
2 Miles South of Delaware Memorial Bridge
NEW CASTLE, DELAWARE

FLORIDA

Florida motels evoke memories of family road trips to the coast, the car hurtling along newly paved interstates in search of sun and beach sand and perhaps a box of oranges to ship to the folks back home. While many motels eek out their existences near the shore, a fairly sizable collection awaits the ambling driver along the old numbered highways like 1, 19, 27, and 301.

If you happen to be on the road at night along Highway 27, passing through Avon Park, you will praise the neon deities at the site of Reed's Motel. A gigantic red arrow points the way while a ramrod-straight diving girl plunges toward invisible waters. Glowing red and blue, the motel offers an immediate test of your road buddies:

Those who think the motel is tacky might just as well get home in time to catch Must See TV.

Heading north, you can search out the tiny motor courts that thrived before the coming of the interstates. The Haines City Motor Court even offered its visitors a poem that speaks to the magic of motor travel in the Sunshine State:

Where the orange groves reach in splendor
To the East and to the West
Where traveler from the Northlands
Find the sun's rays are the best.

Where the tall palm trees in winter
Reach away toward the rising Sun,
There the traveler likes to settle
When his driving is all done.

At the Haines City Court
He will find such peace and rest,
There the cabins are the cleanest
And the bedding is the best.

If your itinerary demands a Westerly drive, make sure you take time for St. Petersburg, postcard City of Green Benches where the Sandman Motel provides an essential stop for motel photographers. The sign features a twinkling figure with a trailing nightcap and bag of sand inviting strangers into the land of nod. Like a street mime or

Tropical Palms Court, Fort Myers, Florida (c)

Olympic gymnast, the figure looks cute at first, but gets creepy after a while. Even so, the rooms provide an inexpensive respite from bay area traffic. Traveling up 19, you will find a dozen or so neon beauties along the quiet stretch of road, many oriented around the town of Perry. Here, the leisurely fantasy of 1950s and 1960s Florida, a land of shuffleboard courts and inexpensive t-shirts, seems to attract the kind of travelers who have never heard of the whip-fast interstate just a few miles away.

If your journey takes you inland toward the city of Gainesville, take extra time to stop by the Florida Motel where mossy trees and dangling palm fronds greet the sweltering days of August with a shrug. Behind the strip of rooms, sunrays drift through the foliage lighting the secret spaces where lizards glare from the walls. Exposed brick and rough stucco offer a subdued response to the jaunty googie-style yellow arrow whose missing light bulbs stopped blinking years ago. The motel's most striking feature, of course, is its sign: an otherwise standard marquee blessed with a metal blue facsimile of the Sunshine State.

GEORGIA

PERRY COURT
PERRY, GA.

The 1996 Olympics did little good for motels in **Georgia**. Unlike the clutches of ancient motor inns that managed to hang on during the hurricane of construction and refurbishment accompanying the Salt Lake City Olympics six years later, Atlanta demolished many of its older motels in a quest to pull its image together for the television cameras. Today when you tour the "City Too Busy to Hate," you'll find plenty of upscale chains but few really nice motels. For relief from the congestion and the plethora of peach tree references, head to Resaca (north of Calhoun on Highway 41) in search of that most beautiful of visions: the glow of an open motel at night. The rooms at the Country Boy Inn are standard with prints of bamboo trees, pea soup colored vinyl chairs, and that indescribable smell that wafts into your nostrils the first time you open the door. In the morning, you'll awaken to the passage of trucks and the splashing of kids in the pool.

Heading to the southwestern corner of the Peach State, you can't miss the Candlelight Motel reclining off Highway 27 in the town of Columbus, home of Fort Benning and the Ranger Training School. Where

else will you find a motel sign shaped like a giant candleholder? Shoot some photos but remember your personal safety. The Candlelight may have once provided a novel stop between monotonous hours of highway driving but its value as a family motel has declined with the economy in these parts. Throughout town, businesses proclaim their love for the troops with yellow ribbons and welcome home signs, but the town also invokes the less gallant side of the military economy with its plethora of pawn shops, payday loan stores, and title buy-back opportunities. For locals who have slipped off the last wrung, a national firm advertises on gaudy billboards, "We Buy Ugly Houses."

Return eastward a bit where red clay marks the curvaceous earth and locals hang hollowed gourds that serve as birdhouses. As is the case throughout the South, many tourist motels have gone to seed, slowly transforming themselves into weekly flophouses. Even so, you'll find nicer digs in the Talbotten Motel, along old U.S. Route 80 where floppy butterflies drift on the breeze and local pickup truck drivers wave to strangers. The Talbotten sleeps alongside the Southern Pacific Highway, a road that extends across the nation from the beaches of San Diego to the gracious gardens of Savannah, an impressive span of 3,000 miles. But in tiny towns like Talbotten, the

road makes no pretense of its grandeur. Harkening back to a time when motels provided a range of services, from greasy cafes to jittery coffee shops and late-night filling stations, the Talbotten Motel features a neighboring trading post that sells unfinished rocking chairs and lawn jockeys from the Age that Political Correctness Forgot. On a Sunday afternoon, you'll be fortunate to find the motel office open for business. But stop anyway to watch the yellow-black locusts crawl through the wet green grass.

HAWAII

Tourists seek out **Hawaii** for its lush rainforests, active volcanoes, and sea turtles – not to mention hula dances, overpriced luaus, and tacky tiki torches. Inexpensive motels do not easily come to mind when visiting the Aloha State, particularly if you limit your excursions to Honolulu. Touring the city's canyons of high-rise hotels and congested streets, you may think you've stumbled into Los Angeles. The fact is if you're searching for Mom and Pop motels whose vernacular architecture reminds you of Polynesian hula fantasies, you'd better stick to mainland coastal cities like Wildwood, New Jersey, where travelers still admire tacky design. Hawaii is too expensive to be kitschy. Might as well head to the Windward Coast in search of Countryside Cabins in Panaluu. The owners pride themselves on their chilled out attitude and the prices accommodate a range of folks, from tourists just off the plane to long-term hikers living out of their duffel bags. Under a cornucopia of swollen fruit with near dizzying ocean views, the Cabins reflect Hawaii's invitation to slow down and savor things a bit.

Even so, part of the problem is that many visitors devote most of their time to Oahu, forgetting that simple pleasures of dirt roads and local diners where folks come to

the *Waikikian*

Hawaii's Most Beautiful Hotel

"talk story" are more easily found on less densely populated islands. You should definitely hop to the green paradise of Kauai. When visiting the island's largest city, Lihue, watch out for the wild chickens that cross the road any time they please and keep an eye peeled for the Tip Top Cafe and Motel. A Lihue tradition for eighty-five years, the Tip Top specializes in island diner food, including banana-macadamia nut pancakes whose aromas attract all manner of local and visiting folks. The rooms, built in 1965 to cash in on the tourist trade, are less memorable. But they are clean and comfortable enough, especially when compared to the budget-buster hotel complexes on the beach. For some readers, the idea of staying in a downtown motel in Hawaii might seem a tad depressing but remember the best beach of your trip is the one just down the road. Beachfront lodgings are almost always overrated.

Naturally, you'll want to visit the Big Island just to see what all the fuss is about. Flying overhead, it's hard not to gasp at the stunning view of molten lava fields and perfect sunsets. However, you may be surprised to know that you're also near the southernmost point in the United States. If you've ever wanted to stay at the southernmost *motel* in the nation, you're in luck. The Shirakawa Motel in Naalehu offers sunny and clean rooms for jaw-droppingly reasonable rates. Getting there takes some patience. You'll need to follow mile markers and remember the rules of the road: never honk your horn unless you're greeting a friend. When you arrive, prepare for a friendly greeting from Mrs. Shirakawa herself. Of course, the furniture is old, you're likely to share a hallway bathroom, and folks here generally don't accept credit cards. But the nearby plantation town is quiet and largely devoid of crowds.

IDAHO

Driving through **Idaho**, you may contemplate rolling rain clouds and rumors about mountain crazies, but drop into Coeur d'Alene on a summer evening and you'll find more than pickup trucks and homemade fishing reels. You'll discover one of the most delightful motels in the nation. The old Flamingo Motel, which has been around for five decades, offers lipstick pink doors, hand stenciled walls, and museum quality appliances and fixtures to spice up theme rooms with names like Ivy, Garden, and Americana. Russ, a fellow from nearby Spokane, still removes quarters from the Magic Fingers box while Fran works hard to maintain her standards:

A lot of people think 'cos it's 50s, it's not gonna be clean and nice, because a lot of 'em aren't. A lot of them don't keep them up. But we really work hard keeping them clean, 'cos we've got time. I don't give my girls a time limit. You don't have only 20 minutes. If you have to take an hour to clean it, I don't care. I want it clean.

Get back onto the road heading east but look sharp or you may just miss the town of Wallace, literally under the shadow of an interstate bypass. Slow down and creep through the town late at night. You can't miss the downtown apartment lined with enough lights for a movie premier. Around here, folks hang tough in the face of depleting silver mines and disappearing jobs. Even so, the blinking lights of the Stardust Motel evoke dreams of better days. With its horizontal strips of plate glass and flagcrete support columns, the motel resembles a 1950s-era blurring of downtown diner and suburban high school.

In Pocatello, the old Idaho Motel with its state-shaped wall has given way to an apartment complex and no one can quite recall the location of the even more ancient Rainbow Cottage Camp that offered gas plates and coal stoves in cabins priced for a

I'D RATHER VACATION AT...
FLAMINGO MOTEL

buck. Heading south along U.S. 30, slow down to catch a breather in Soda Springs. One morning, you might pass through a gauntlet of flag waving patriots demonstrating their support for troops fighting overseas. On the site of Mormon pioneer Brigham Young's summer home, you can stay at the Brigham Young Lodge. Nearby, on the marquee of the local sandwich shop, one fellow has asked, "Clara Will U Go 2 Prom With Me?" A second line below, presumably unrelated, reads: "Breakfast 8 AM."

Head toward Twin Falls and stop by the Amber Motel. During our visit, we find a woman resembling a refugee from that Edward Hopper painting sitting in a plastic chair under the long shadows of the setting sun. Staring out over the interstate, she waits as cars stream toward the twinkling lights. Farther into town, the El Rancho is located across the street from a Dairy Queen. The owner has bought and sold the motel a few times but has decided to hunker down. Inside, Glinda manages the desk while also unclogging the pipes, answering the phones, and caring for her granddaughter. Waking after six, crashing after midnight, Glinda has pretty much organized her life around the comings and goings of strangers.

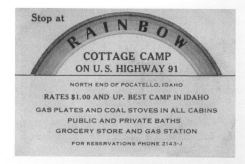

ILLINOIS

Perhaps the best way to enter **Illinois** is to cruise in from the north where Highway 30 meets the Great River Road. If you arrive during the summer, you might notice a brown and white painted sign for the Pine Motel planted in a cornfield. A mile down the road, pull into this treasure located in the town of Fulton and chat a while with the owners, Dale and Darlene Ketelsen. While they take pride in the local recognition that their court has received, they'll tell you that running a family motel is a job that never ends: "It's a 24-hour operation here," Darlene sighs. "Come in at two o'clock in the morning and we still answer the doorbell."

The road from Fulton to Chicago traverses a typically quiet section of the old Lincoln Highway, now labeled U.S. 30. As you roll down the windows to catch a whiff of the country air, you zip by the ruins of tourist courts that once advertised tiny cabins and green lawns. In Rock Falls, you spot the brick-red awnings and y-posts of a motel soon to become a memory while the road heading for Shabbona reveals an almost perfectly preserved tourist court sign whose grey and white arrow points toward ghostly memories. Just before Chicago, visit the nice folks at the Shady Lawn Motel, the one that advertises "TV" in that neo-electrical lettering that once seemed to spark

with exotic energies. But don't plan to stay; the Shady Lawn has become an apartment complex.

In the Chicago-Rockford metroplex, check out the Brer Rabbit Motel in Villa Park, a suburb of the Windy City. One of the most photographed motel signs in Illinois, the Brer Rabbit offers a pleasant rest from the highway with its tree-lined rooms bordered by tiny postage stamp lawns, each immaculately maintained. Further west in Rockford, the Rustic Motel manages to hold on despite the cars that whiz by unaware of its charms. While we photograph the site, a little girl in a blue sundress dances in the driveway waving an American flag. As her blonde pigtails sway in the breeze, the Rustic appears at once to be a little brighter than it was before.

Finally, if you plan to cross Illinois via the National Road that stretches from east St. Louis straight to the Indiana border, seek out the relic sign of the former Rainbo Court, close to the Cahokia Mounds Historic Site. While the motel has assumed a new identity in recent years, you may still discern the outline of a marquee that has confused many a highway wanderer searching for a classic Holiday Inn "Great Sign." Further east, spend a bit more time in Greenup ("Village of the Porches") on your way out of the state. Chances are you'll want to stay at the 5 Star Motel. Its owners, Dennis and Kathryn Stites, have maintained this calm and comfortable motel for years. Pay careful attention. Given its location under a lush overhang of trees, the motel seems to disappear from the road. Keep your eyes open, though. It's worth the search.

Finding a good motel in the Hoosier State is a test of endurance. Along many of **Indiana**'s numbered highways, tourist courts and motor lodges have given up the ghost, knuckling under the pressure of chain behemoths or slipping into the twilight of short-term apartment complexes or long-term flophouses. However, in Fort Wayne, you'll find one friendly place worth the hassle of getting there: The Pine Haven Motel. On the breezeway toward the lobby, you'll also find a tiny marigold garden oriented around a flock of plastic ducks.

If you're heading west with plans to attend the great Ligonier Marshmallow Festival on Labor Day, you might stay at the nearby Goshen Motor Lodge. When you arrive in town, the Goshen sign leaps into your sight with bouncing square letters and twinkling stars atop the Motor Inn moniker, a tad tacky for this region but friendly enough all the same. After picking toasted white goo out of your hair and

clothes from the Marshmallow Fest, settle back in this Indiana backroads community where Amish buggies and verdant farmland remind you that very little of the United States may be found on television.

Before long, you return to the road, searching for fortune in Indianapolis by way of Highway 31. You'll drift past impossibly

ornate houses, monsters of plaster, iron, and mass produced confidence. Contemplating the shift in architecture as you enter the metropolitan region, you recall that motels generally reside in a ring around large cities, off the old blue highways, just within the arc of auto superstores and subdivisions built upon formerly cheap farmland, what city folks once called "the country." However, the push of urban renewal chewed up the smaller motels in the margin between downtown and suburbia. At one point, the Beauty Park Tourist Cabins stood on the old National Highway

through town. The Cabins offered "a Safe Place for Ladies Traveling Alone," all for a buck per person. Of course, that was when motels advertised new-fangled technologies like steam heat and long distance service.

Turn east on Highway 40, passing beat up remnants like the Gem Motel, before turning south on Highway 52. You slow down a bit as the rains begin to fall and the little towns through which you pass curl themselves around tighter and windier curves of the Whitewater River. Preparing to abandon your search, threatening to drop into neighboring Ohio with a nasty temper, you then catch sight of the long thin line of red neon about three miles south of Brookville: The Mound Haven Motel. This motel reminds you of what you search for in Mom and Pop operations: an owner who looks you in the eye when taking your money, a room that hasn't suffered the insult of modernization, and a television that seems to only get the *Andy Griffith Show*. With its clean sheets and comfy bed, the Mound Haven energizes you for another day on the road.

can study the horizon for a quieter, nicer abode less than fifteen miles east of town. Slow down when you reach the Motel 20 in Moville. Located along a frontage road, the motel offers a humble attempt at theme rooms including one dedicated to the 1950s, a jacuzzi room, and one oriented around a cola-flavored soft drink that ought not be mentioned here. Trademark lawyers get enough business without our help. The Motel 20 aligns itself with a cafe small and local enough not to need a name.

For many folks greeting **Iowa** for the first time along Highway 20, Sioux City provides their initial glimpse of the Hawkeye State. And that's not necessarily a good thing. The city's local, non-canned country station goes by the call letters KSUX, for goodness sake. By night, the city burns with the otherworldly glow of "Riverboat" gambling while old roadside motels slowly decay. By morning you might drop by the Corey Motel with its little stone block cabins, each shaded by an individual tree. Nearby a massive grain complex fills a line of trains just passing through.

Before long, the chug of morning traffic releases you into the countryside and you

Farther east you'll find the Sac City Motel, appropriately enough located in Sac City. The motel achieves what its owner, Sky Nyblom, dreamed of when he traveled the country. Sky said, "I've stayed in more motels than most people have seen.... So I made the motel the way I wanted when I was traveling." Running a most quintessential Mom and Pop motel, Sky has crafted just about every tacky tourist trinket to remind folks of his lodge: pencils, combs, postcards, and other doodads. When not thinking up ways to attract guests, Sky is happy to help clean birds brought in by local hunters. And folks dropping in from out of town to attend a local wedding often receive hand painted flowerpots as a memento of their stay. Before you leave, don't forget to say hello to Luke the Birddog.

Of course, if your Iowa entry leaps northeast from Omaha, Nebraska, along the Lincoln Highway, there's one essential stop in the town of Denison: The Park Motel.

Recently placed on the National Register of Historic Places, the Spanish colonial-style Park recalls the days when the nearby highway first reflected the dreams of motorists setting out in search of adventure. Shuffling off from the anonymous city, one could envision a journey to distant places by pulling into this midwestern hacienda. Today's visitors who still remember Donna Reed from *It's a Wonderful Life* and *From Here to Eternity* will also delight to stay in the Donna Reed theme room at the Park. Donna Reed was, after all, a Denison native.

Finally, if you find yourself in eastern Iowa in search of the *Field of Dreams* site in Dyersville (They built it — will you come?), hold out for the Terrace Motel in nearby Dubuque. Overlooking Highway 20, the two-story brick building offers a metal sign bolted to the front door that bespeaks the owner's love of history: "American Motor Hotel Association, Serving Motels since 1941."

KANSAS

Throughout the country, you'll find a few mystical convergences of classic design, friendly folks, and glowing neon. One such place, easily one of the most beautiful roadside photography opportunities in the plains, awaits in Salina, **Kansas**, where the street of Broadway weaves around a gorgeous arc of glowing wonders, including the Starlight, the Airliner, and the Budget King. The Log Cabin Motel invites you to ponder the twilight as the sky blurs from blue to pink to black. An L-shaped motel with white steel chairs, the Log Cabin invites weary motorists to duck in from the highway grime, not to mention a neon-lit cabin that earns the motel's namesake.

East of Salina, The Simmer Motel represents an essential stop for lovers of family-owned motels. Once known as the New Look Motel, the Simmer offers the most comfortable bed the authors of this book have occupied while on the road.

We met Cheri Simmer a little past midnight one evening when she greeted us in her bathrobe, wiping sleep from her eyes. It takes little prodding to inspire Cheri to pour forth her ten year story of gutted rooms and maxed credit cards as she and her husband have renovated their beloved motor court. Their motel faces the threat of a national chain hotel just across the

THESE SIGNS GO TOGETHER

MOTEL
STEAM HEAT
NO VACANCIES

street. Having saturated the larger markets, many have begun to clone themselves in smaller towns to buy up the reunion and wedding party trade, pushing out the Mom and Pops in the same manner as Wal-Mart has gutted main streets from coast to coast. Even so, Cheri persists in the hope that her motel can endure, painting murals and upgrading furniture: "This is me. And that's why I take it so personally. I've actually been in tears over someone not liking it. Because they want The

SHANGRI LA
DODGE CITY *Motel* KANSAS

Hampton. And we aren't anything like that. And we never will be — and we never pretend to be."

Taking U.S. 24 further east toward Topeka, you'll find the relic of the Sunflower Motel. As morning light creeps through the trees, photographers may strain to capture the cheerful countenance of the Kansas state flower. But the image is worth the wait.

In Kansas City, stop by the White Haven Motor Lodge, which began when Hugh White got fed up with the dairy business and decided to try his hand in the hospitality industry. But if you prefer a site more removed from the downtown hustle, check out the Crest Motel just west of town. Since her mom decided she'd had enough, Christie has managed to do some good in her little place in the world. Regarding her clientele, she says, "It ranges from older people who just need a place to stop over to ladies who get thrown out of their houses with their kids that need a place to stay for a week . . . . I've had a chance to help some folks out. I've also been kinda stabbed in the back a few times. But there's always that one person who ends up coming back and paying the money they owe you — renews your faith to give somebody else a chance."

KENTUCKY

As good a way to pass through **Kentucky** as any, the old U.S. numbered Highway 60 courses through bluegrass country, past tiny cash crops of tobacco and insanely opulent nouveau-riche homes designed to look as if they've stood for decades. The state capital, Frankfort, emerges suddenly like a drop-in guest you haven't seen in a while. Dwarfed by Kentucky's larger cities, the capital offers a small station along the pilgrimage in search of roadside motels. The Anchor Inn Motel has a brick line of wooden doors, each a little different than the other. The doors reflect different stages of the motel's maintenance. By the doors, there are several types of chairs and bench-

es. Years ago, someone was inspired to paint black anchors on some of the bench-es, back when the motel had a couple of steel hanging signs and a fancy neon atten-tion-getter. Today, as daily tenants give way to weekly and monthly stays, no one notices the faded signs anymore.

Continuing west, you might notice an odd convergence of town names along the highway: Shelbyville and Simpsonville. Followers of the hit animated cartoon *The Simpsons* will recall Shelbyville as the neighboring rival of Springfield. Of course, even if you've never caught a single episode, you'll be glad you dropped by the Shelby Motel where Joe and Sandy Russell run a swell operation. Once a farmhouse, the Shelby became a motel when the origi-nal owners added wings to the impressive center span that, even now, boasts four stately white columns holding up a high gable. Taking a moment to chat with a vis-itor, Sandy laughs easily and holds your gaze with sharp blue eyes. Having a no-nonsense attitude about her business, she remains a dedicated believer in the Shelby: "You have to love it, because you're here twenty-four hours a day, seven days a week."

Eventually, your motel pilgrimage will lead you to Cave City, so named because of the cavernous tourist traps nearby. It's

renowned for its Wigwam Village. One of the three Native American-theme motels that remain from the small chain built by Frank Redford, the Village allows you to sleep in a surprisingly spacious teepee and even shop for gifts and curios in the motel gift shop. Generally by early evening, all the rooms are booked. As the sun begins to set, bemused adults relax as children romp in the playground or stare at the cows in the nearby pasture. Turning off the road without calling ahead, you'll probably miss

your chance to follow the motel's slogan and "sleep in a teepee," so plan ahead. Otherwise, other Cave City motels offer plenty of reasonable accommodations and, at one, a chance for redemption. You see, Alan and Joanie Grimes' Caveland Motel doubles as a non-denominational church for travelers whose weariness goes down to the soul. Behind the office, a tiny sanctuary awaits where you'll find services, revivals, and even healings. Strong believers in prophesy, Joanie tells the authors of this book that even their presence reflects God's will: to spread the good news of this unique motel ministry.

LOUISIANA

With its swampy expanses, boiled crawfish, and Cajun patois, a visit to **Louisiana** sometimes seems like a trip to another world. The shadows of Huey Long and Anne Rice cast themselves long over the Pelican State. Of course, judging by the seemingly ubiquitous billboards that advertise gaming (the state slogan could be "if you or anyone you know has a gambling problem …"), as well as the acrid tang of petrochemicals, you might assume that Baton Rouge is little more than a wholly owned subsidiary of the gambling and oil industries.

Driving into town along Highway 61, you pass by a range of deteriorating motels, including one of the remaining Alamo Plaza motels. Once a small chain of courts designed to evoke images of the Texas landmark, the now independently owned motels have largely become dangerous and depressing. In contrast, when you pull through the overhang of the Shades Motel, you enter a fairly nice reminder of family oriented motor inns from the age when 61 was the main road from Louisiana's capital city to New Orleans. The pool is gone and bullet resistant glass separates you from the lobby, but the rooms are nicely appointed. Nearing the midnight hour, the night manager explains, "We spend a lot on paint, carpet, furniture, and that sort of thing. It's an expensive process but nobody's gonna stop if it looks like a rat hole."

Head toward New Orleans, taking 61, and you'll encounter waves of postwar motels, mostly abandoned to the land of hourly rates and soggy carpets. Drop by the town of Metairie to visit the Deep South Motel whose metal trellis railings could have been lifted off a more fashionable stop on Bourbon Street. The old road, here called Airline Highway, also rolls by the Sugar Bowl Courts, a tiny square of pink-sided, green-doored rooms surrounding a gravel lot. Atop the doors, curved "eyebrows," the type you'd find in Miami's South Beach, complete the streamlined moderne scene. Stop for photos, but don't plan on spending the night. Inside the lobby, you face a two-way mirror, no sight of the desk clerk, and enjoy the opportunity to buy a condom for a buck. Heading toward the Big Easy, squint your eyes a bit and you may catch the ghostly images of motels long gone, including the Alto Tourist Court with its stylish portholes and Paradise Tourist Court with its arched overhang that once admitted travelers to quiet bungalows.

Loop back west toward Lafayette, but take the slow road when U.S. 90 transforms itself into an interstate. At the Teche Motel, you'll meet Claude and Rosie Viator whose sixty-four-year-old cabins include a tiny barber shop and a homemade "bayou garden" intended as the couple's retirement project. Mentioned in James Lee Burke's book, *Jolie Blon's Bounce*, the motel hardly seems an appropriate setting for a murder mystery. Yet, it takes little imagination to place its dark shadows and tiny cabins within the novel's gruesome story. Farther along the road, Teresa awaits at the Royal Motel in New Iberia: "Everybody likes each other around here. It's quiet. No trouble."

ALTO TOURIST COURT

Located on U. S. 90 - 6 Miles West of business district.

New Orleans' Most Modern.

MAINE

The **Maine** coast compels you to slow down a bit as you pass through charming fishing towns whose families have worked the waters for generations. Near Kennebunk the aptly named Turnpike Motel provides a decent resting spot before you set off for points north. Built circa 1947, the motel started its life as a house and farmstead before the original owner added a line of rooms to accommodate the travelers appearing on the newly built freeway. Managing the Turnpike with her husband, Don Bridges, Noreen describes life in a family-owned motel: "There's good points and there's bad points. The good point is that you're home. You don't have to travel. The bad point is that you're confined. If you want to leave, you've got to make sure you've got coverage." Her family's not alone, though. Their lobby provides a home to several gorgeous "PR" cats whose thick, lustrous coats earn praise on many of the comment cards the owners receive.

Continuing northward along U.S. Route 1, take extra care to slow down near the Maine Idyll Motor Court near Freeport; you don't want to miss this one. Built by Depression-era laborers, the cabin has provided a quiet night's sleep for three generations — each under the management of the Marstaller family. While chipmunks scamper underfoot, you slip into and out of shadows painted by swaying trees and the darting sun. Later when you step into an office filled with family pictures, you might chat with the current owner, Lewis, who offers a mimeographed poem that has guided his family's stewardship of the Maine Idyll: "To all who travel on life's road of pleasure and pain: / You who stop here should forget your troubles and griefs, your feuds and hates… / May your stay at the Maine Idyll be as a day of sunshine, / new courage, friendship, and hope." One other thing: when you pull into the Idyll and find a local worker singing while he tends to the cabins, don't be alarmed. Folks tend to get musical around here.

Perhaps the most essential stop on your tour of Maine motels is the, well, Maine Motel in Lewiston. Some historians say this is the oldest continually run lodge in the state, begun in the 1920s as Jackson's Pine Cone Cabins and later renamed Grant's Tourist Court. The current owners, Penny and Don Pitt, came to Maine as refugees of New Jersey's growing traffic and troubled economy. The Pitts have begun an extensive research project on their property, discovering that the motel once boast-

4. AT OLD ORCHARD BEACH

ed a luncheonette and gas station. Black and white postcards reveal old style gravity gas pumps and a tiny office that was eventually converted into one of the cabins. Today, you'll only find rooms — each a tiny bit different from the others. A few years after buying their motel in the country, the Pitts work to modernize their motel without destroying its rich past. Driving by, you'll have no difficulty spotting the property thanks to the red Adirondack chairs near each cabin.

MARYLAND

Ocean City marks the beginning of **Maryland**'s Highway 50, more than 3,000 miles from its Western terminus in Sacramento. Crossing through Washington D.C., Highway 50, often called the Loneliest Highway, launches through a vast range of territory from the Virginia Shenandoah Valley, through the Missouri Ozarks, deep into the painted canyons of Utah, and toward the golden shores of California. It passes through a dozen states in all. Starting in Ocean City, you face a bewildering array of Oceanside motels.

The Nassau Motel offers as nice a set of lodgings as you'll find near the water. With vibrant orange doors and cool green railings, the Nassau offers a jaunty vision of Caribbean sun and sand even when a few summer rains begin to fall. Be careful if you plan to visit in June, though. The Nassau offers special deals for high school seniors and, rumor has it, some of them like to party hard.

If your interests veer toward quieter pursuits, head inland toward the Alamo Court to start your journey along Highway 50. Said to be the oldest motel in Ocean City, this roadside gem was built in 1945 to accommodate the throngs of travelers hitting the two-lane to all points west. Borrowing the pueblo styling of a southwestern mission, complete with wooden beams sticking out from a stucco-like facade, the Alamo offers an ersatz history lesson for the price of a night's lodging. This is, after all, a motel. Even so, the new owners have set up a tiny grill and have big plans for their property. But the motel will surely outlive even them and their new slogan, "Bring Your Ass to the Alamo."

Also, in case you're curious, the motel has no connection to the Alamo Courts and Plazas founded by E. Lee Torrance. He was a guy who soundly rejected the use of nighttime lighting to draw customers. "No

Finally, here's a story from a few years ago when we found ourselves on Highway 50, heading west from Ocean City. Leaving the congested heart of the city we spotted the Pines Motel across from a mall that once was a cornfield. Sure enough, the sign featured two pines, but they were painted white. We eventually learned that an extra shade of green would have cost the owner too much. Under the sign that said, "Office," the Pines once advertised Air Conditioning and Cable TV. Frank, the owner, was more than willing to explain what happened: "I took them down. Wanna know why? Because people'd come in and say, 'Hey, you got air conditioning and cable?' And I got so sick of making 'em look ignorant, saying 'look at the sign' that I took 'em down." Apparently those questions got Frank a little annoyed and he ended up closing the Pines for good.

sir, no neon," Torrance once announced. "We don't want to look like a beer joint." (quoted in *The Motel in America* by Jakle, Sculle, and Rogers) To the delight of photographers for half a century, this Alamo features a neon sign that would have earned Torrance's wrath. Go ahead and stay anyway; he'll never know.

Massachusetts represents two clashing ideals of highway travel. As workers and engineers struggle to complete Boston's Big Dig in an effort to reduce the arterial clog that grinds Beantown traffic to a standstill for much of the day, Highway 1 meanders through the urban maze in a dancing time warp of Eisenhower-era signage and quirky architectural design. Sadly, the famed vacation road that connected states along the Eastern Seaboard, laid out near the remnants of the colonial post roads, loses much of its character when confronted with the interstate construction and urban "renewal" of the Boston metroplex. Seeking a motel in the Bay State's capital city is an exercise in frustration as rates are insanely high. Yet slightly north in Saugus, you'll find nicer accommodations and a bit of history as well. Organizations such as the local Saugus Historical Society are working to add classic stopovers like the Ferns "air conditioned" motel and the nearby Chisholm Motel to the National Register of Historic Places. Through their efforts, tourist courts that have marked time since the 1920s (in the case of the faded Ferns) might yet endure.

If you're looking for a place to stay, though, seek out the Chisholm Motel. The 1930s-era Chisholm stands despite the belief that aging courts represent a blighting influence to be avoided by tourists seeking only the newest and most modern accommodations. The old sign with its elongated M forming the border of san-serif letters that continue to glow a soft pink has seen its share of history. The lights of the intersecting arrow no longer work and the whole sign seems ready to collapse on itself. To attract wary motorists, the motel once built a nicer sign along the road, but nothing quite replaces the origi-

BEST CAMPS
COURTS AND LODGES
CANADA TO MEXICO

"The end of a perfect day and a perfectly comfortable stopping place"

RECOMMENDED BY

COMPILED BY
BEST CAMPS ASSOCIATION
Copyright—Best Camps   LITHO IN U.S.A.

Arrow Gift Shop and Cabins on the Mohawk Trail, at Charlemont, Mass.

one last time to see the Arns Park Motel. Located in North Attleboro, the Arns lobby resembles nothing less than a highway cathedral with its A-frame grandeur and stained glass windows that shed gracious light on the reception desk. Just old enough to continue to advertise itself and its touchtone phones as "ultramodern," the Arns Park demonstrates one tiny victory for the ideal of highway travel that means searching for somewhere different.

nal. When you're in town, drop by the Hilltop Restaurant for a steak. You can't miss the eighty-foot-tall glowing cactus.

Head south of Boston, just past the New England Patriots Gillette Stadium, and visit the Red Fox Motel. As the business marches along a depressing decline from nightly vacation rates to weekly apartment rents, the motel maintains some of its dignity with a colonial-style lobby complete with white pillars. In comical contrast, the motel's logo features a grinning fox that may remind you of Saturday morning cartoons when a dumb-struck doofus catches sight of a "foxy dame." Its logo's eyes bulged and tongue agog, the Red Fox Motel still manages a sense of humor about itself and its fate.

Before departing Massachusetts for the commercial and industrial canyons of Providence, Rhode Island, slip off Route 1

MICHIGAN

THE ELMS MOTEL
South Dort Highway on U.S. 10, Flint, Michigan

Like most northern states, **Michigan** often serves as the departure site for highway motorists heading toward warmer climes. However, with a little patience you can find some pretty cool motels in the Wolverine State. When driving through Detroit, beat-up capital of America's nearly pulverized auto industry, you might need a bit more patience than you think. On Michigan's eastern terminus of Highway 12, Detroit dares you to find a nice motel along its weather-beaten roadside strip. Purple-neon "gentlemen's clubs" and all night massage parlors compete for your attention, glaring their wares next to motels like the Travel-Log and Mercury Motel. Keep heading west and you'll drop a couple extra bucks on the Fellow's Creek Motel. The rooms, suites really, have been recently updated with showy furniture and comfy beds.

Farther down the road, you'll notice a peculiar shadow cast by the sign for the De Swan Motel. That's right, it's a huge wind-

mill — a reflection on the region's Scandinavian heritage and its willingness to feed the fantasies of highway travelers itching to feel that they've actually gone somewhere. Unfortunately, the motel has seen better days. It now sags under the shadow of a row of pour trucks for a concrete company, greeting its visitors with aluminum foil covered windows, cracked pavement and a dumpster on the green. Drop by but don't plan on staying too long.

Still driving late at night? Grit your teeth and follow the 12 on its leisurely course southward from Interstate 94. As the stars turn overhead, you recall a fable of a motel with a giant neon soldier that salutes visitors to his motel. You pass by ancient barns

that have been transformed into antique shops, used bookstores that work on the honor system, and the odd leprechaun advertising a series of tourist traps combined into Irish Hills. Gulp down the grainy last drops of coffee you bought hours ago at Tim Hortons and look over your left shoulder. Was that a muffler man transformed into Paul Bunyan? Another "Mystery Hill" farther down the road?

As the moon continues to rise, ease into the friendly town of Coldwater and look to your right. Sure enough, a metal soldier lifts a mechanical neon hand, saluting your arrival to the Cadet Motor Inn. Perhaps the lobby may still be open. The Cadet

opened in 1963 as an investment and, particularly in the past decade, has become a genuine Mom and Pop motel. Starting in their early twenties, Matt and Jenny Stritzinger refurbished the Cadet, tossing out the drug dealers and prostitutes, and removing the tacky facade, opening the rooms to the outside, befitting an authentic roadside motel. The Stritzingers have had plenty of franchise opportunities, folks from the highway chains looking to bolt their plastic logo onto the prime location. Matt refuses their entreaties every time: "If I'm gonna run my own business, I don't need somebody in a franchise sticking their nose in, telling me what I want to do and don't want to do."

MINNESOTA

Minnesota earns its nicknames (North Star State and Land of 10,000 Lakes) for its icy climate and plentiful waters, but you'll also find an assortment of under recognized, tacky roadside attractions built, it seems, simply to stave off boredom. Starting your drive from the twin cities, take a moment to savor the Northernaire Motel in Maplewood, just off Highway 61 (yes, the same one that plunges southwardly through a nation of Blues toward New Orleans). Walking into the lobby of the Northernaire, you'll find an aerial view — photograph of the V-shaped site aligning the highway. Think of the time and effort needed to procure such an image, and con-

sider the pride and concern taken in the construction of this motel. Really. Would anyone care to see an overhead view of a cloverleaf Holiday Inn? Today, white Christmas lights line the rooms and the red sign looks more than a little weather-beaten, but you can't escape the simple truth of the motel's slogan: "We Sell Sleep!"

Heading west toward Willmar, don't blink or you'll miss the Hi-Way12 Motel. The rooms are nice enough and you can't beat the location — across the street from a genuinely old-school Dairy Queen (no "DQ" around here). Even so, the selection of this motel for placement in a book about roadside Mom and Pop lodgings caused some consternation among the authors. One asserts that a boring prefab orange sign would almost instantly disqualify the motel from consideration. The other, in a somewhat more wistful mood, proposes that any motel willing to maintain the name of an old numbered highway, particularly one that has not been transformed into a commercial advertising totem, deserves a little love. Drop by and decide for yourself.

Heading north a bit toward Alexandria, check out the Skyline Motel, the one with a giant wood-log, swinging bench, and a painted sign featuring a silhouette of tall birches under a silvery white moon next to

In case the Skyline doesn't grab you, keep heading north toward Fergus Falls in search of the giant otter. These folks take living in Otter Tail county seriously; they built a climbable forty-foot otter in a park along the main road. Heaven help us if a nearby city decides to wage an otter war by building a larger one. One "world's largest otter" is clearly enough. Not too far away, you might drop by the Motel 7 where they offer free popcorn in the lobby. Of course, given the accumulation of anonymous chain motels that have crept into town in recent years, they have to entice guests anyway they can.

Before heading out of state toward North Dakota (don't turn back, the state is worth your time!), head into Dilworth where you might find Bill Ponovand repairing the glass letters of his Star-Lite Motel. He'd just as soon take the sign down ("Each letter is $125 if I break them," he says, shaking his head ruefully. "And I break them."). The only problem is too many photographers stream by to take pictures of his sign and he doesn't have the heart to let them down.

the office. Sitting on the picnic table next to a grill (an all-too-rare amenity provided by motels these days), a long wide expanse of doors and windows is broken by occasional red begonias below a perfectly blue sky that stretches out over the prairies beyond. For city dwellers, the smaller towns of the great northern states offer an awesome display of calm.

MISSISSIPPI

Paul Simon offers an apt introduction to the Magnolia State in a song depicting his journey into the heart of the Blues: "The **Mississippi** Delta was shining like a national guitar. I am following the river, down the highway through the cradle of the Civil War." On your journey northward along the famed Highway 61, you will encounter a state struggling to find its way in the "New South" as it confronts economic and demographic changes. But you'll also meet folks who've run their businesses for decades and manage to offer a kind word to every stranger they meet.

Driving north on 61 from Natchez to Vicksburg, you'll find the usual chain opportunities, but few genuinely memorable stays. One unique motel, however, is the Battlefield Inn. Once a franchise operation but now independently owned, the Battlefield reflects the architectural equivalent of a mullet haircut: formal lobby in front, casual rooms in the back. Of course, the Battlefield never takes itself too seriously, as evidenced by its dozens of humorous billboards like, "Stay awhile. Grant did." Nevertheless, you'll find plenty of reasons to stay including a number of colorful (and loud) parrots, a mini-golf course, and proximity to one of the most important Civil War battlefields in the country.

Detouring away from the river toward the

JONES MOTEL
Air Conditioned
U. S. 49 — Collins, Miss.

capital city of Jackson, you might follow U.S. 80 across the city's southern flank. Several of the motels offer photographic opportunities, most notably the Redwood Court on the east side of the blue highway. But beware the dangerous environs, only slightly less scary than the barbed wire prison encampment of the Tarrymore Motel nearby. Best head north again, perhaps through Yazoo City along highway 49 or, better yet, toward Winona at the crossroads of 82 and 51.

A quick passage through Winona offers little more than some gas stations to the harried motorist. Like all too many southern towns, it makes little effort to hide its poverty from passing eyes. Near the crossroads, the Hitching Post Motor Inn sits upon an expansive parking lot empty of cars. Hanging from the motel's 1960s era Holiday-Inn-like facade, Christmas lights dangle in the summer heat. Behind the motel, a windy road climbs over a leafy

hill, passing by election posters for incorruptible sheriffs (they promise).

Pushing a westerly course toward the river, stop by Clarksdale at the crossroads of Highways 49 and 61 where one blues musician reportedly sold his soul to the devil in return for supernatural talent. There, you might search out the old Greyhound bus terminal that features a neon dog galloping through the night. If the road has depleted your endurance, drop into Hicks Motel. There may be fancier digs in town, most notably the Plantation Inn, but the Hicks is cheaper and still manages to offer a decent accommodation. Plus, there's something nearly mystical about a motel sign whose arrow appears to contain dozens of fireflies pointing the way to a respectable night's sleep. A final burn north and you'll cruise into Memphis just over the state line. Somewhere, Elvis Presley is ordering a peanut butter and banana sandwich.

Little King's
HOTEL COURT
HOT WATER HEAT

U.S. Highway 66 ★ WEST OF MAIN STREET
JOPLIN, MO.

You can find any number of trails across the Show Me State, but Route 66 from St. Louis to Joplin offers "the highway that's the best." Crossing and recrossing **Missouri**'s Interstate 44, the Mother Road drifts through tiny towns like Doolittle (named for the commander of the famed World War II raid) and Cuba whose historic murals offer the second best reason to stop in this tiny town of flags and friendly faces. The first reason to stop? The Wagon Wheel Motel, run by Pauline and Harold since 1963. Recently placed on the National Register of Historic Places, the Wagon Wheel was built by a German architect whose design was inspired by the stone cottages of his youth. Built from local Ozark stone, the Wagon Wheel looks

as if a European fairyland of cottages has been dropped into the green hills of rural America.

Continue southwest toward Rolla and look hard. You might just spot the decay of John's Modern Cabins as the sun sets through a canopy of trees. The six cabins (and two nearby outhouses) have suffered from decades of neglect, and the red sign that promises a piece of motel modernity reflects only mournful irony as cars scream by. But the 1930s-era cabins offer a photographer's dream — if you visit soon. A fan planted Burma Shave-like signs nearby that read: "Photograph these while you're here. The wrecking ball is looming near."

Head farther south toward Lebanon and you'll have more luck with the Munger Moss Motel whose sign advertises, "Here yesterday, today, and tomorrow." Bob and Ramona Lehman maintain this Mother Road classic out of love for the people who keep the road alive. Ramona explains, "They're just good people. They're humble people. And it's like one big family that keeps growing and growing and growing and you care about 'em — and they care about you." Working at the Munger Moss since 1971, Ramona takes great pride in her motel. She has started to develop theme rooms, including one for each of the eight states linked by Route 66. However, the coolest theme belongs to the Coral Court Room, dedicated to the famed St. Louis landmark replaced by tract housing a few years back. With its pink and black tile and satin sheets, this room would fit nicely in any bordello — a perfect homage to the famed No-Tell Motel.

To the west, Highway 36 brings you to Stewartsville where a vision from the 1950s and 1960s rises over the hill: a giant multi-pointed star hoisted aloft on a pole. Occupying a special place within the pantheon of goofy motifs, this "sputnik" reflects a strange Cold War fascination and fear of space age imagery. How odd that the sputnik starburst along with crossed ovals of nuclear radiation would become a motif for "space age" design! They're getting harder to find these years, but the Startlight Motel hasn't forgotten its past. The only problem is there's no motel there anymore. The rooms now belong to a pizza joint, a country notions store, and even a CPA. Progress.

MONTANA

With its gurgling streams, distant peaks, and mammoth clouds, **Montana** stretches out in all directions, easily earning its nickname, Big Sky Country. From the west along Interstate 90, drop into Missoula, picking up the eastern stretch of the business route that once went by the name of U.S. 12. There, the Bel Aire Motel offers a clean double-decker with strips of garish pink neon. Get your room there but don't forget to check out the City Center Motel next door where a neon bear snoozes among glowing trees and a smiling moon. Ranking high in the category of must-photograph motel signs in the northwest, the City Center deserves a quick stop.

Farther east beyond Butte, the dusty town of Whitehall calls you to encounter the Chief Motel. With its caricatured native wearing colorful feathers and a stern visage,

the Chief almost always earns a gasp when viewed next to the motel's slogan, "Me Like Um." The nearby tiki torches surrounding the curved gravel parking lot confirm that cultural sensitivity has not yet come to town. Even so, one wonders at the power of "exotic" imagery to fire the imaginations of American motorists and, perhaps, even inspire them to stray from their own reservations.

Of course, if you're looking for a comfortable night's stay free of these sorts of philosophical dalliances, head to Bozeman and the family-owned Royal 7 Motel. Here you encounter another "great sign" similar to the Holiday Inn that never quite fell out of fashion with lovers of fifties and sixties roadside motels. Plan to arrive soon, though, because the city wants them to tear the sign down. Apparently some folks have a problem with the fact that The Royal greets its visits with a marquee three

MONTANA

times bigger than current city ordinances — and it flashes to boot. Curses! The owner vows to hold out as long as he can and will probably succeed as long as he doesn't file a permit for any new construction. One other essential detail about Bozeman: If you want to stare down piles of succulent beef, pork, and bratwurst served on a wooden cutting board, follow your nose to the Bar 3 BBQ in town. It's easily some of the best meat you'll eat on the road.

Continuing south along U.S. 89, head for the majestic Yellowstone National Park. The roadbed — bumper to bumper with cars, vans, and RVs — is a nesting spot for nature lovers on photographic shooting sprees. The mule deer, bull moose, bison, and other beasts are all fair game for inquisitive shutterbugs. It's not uncommon around here to see well intended, though somewhat misguided, activists screaming, "Give 'em space!," from a gas guzzling, ozone depleting metal dinosaur. Sure you can plant a tent near waterfalls and moonlit rivers, but you can enjoy an authentic experience with nature before even entering the park, too. In the town of Gardiner, right near the entrance to Yellowstone, the Hillcrest Cabins have been known to provide grounds for wandering elk, deer, and even buffalo.

NEBRASKA

Nebraska comes by its Cornhusker nickname honestly, at least. You may travel a thousand miles and never see so much corn in your life. Of course, you also may never enjoy the opportunity to drive such a wonderfully preserved stretch of the Lincoln Highway as when you tackle the length from Bushnell to Omaha. Along the way, you may find packs of "wanderfreundes" (hiking friends) who have chosen to walk various lengths of Highway 30.

They've formed a Nebraska organization and distribute patches to folks who've endured/enjoyed certain stretches of the old road. Chances are these friendly folks can direct you to a great motel nearby.

In Sidney, the Lincoln Highway eases past the El Palomino Motel, a streamlined beauty that would appear from overhead as a Flash Gordon flying ship with rooms located along two long wings and an office for the cockpit. Painted orange and brown with yellow doors, the spaceship would find its home base somewhere in the Southwest but simply must have run out of jet fuel in the plains states. They don't get a lot of fancy tourists around here but they do have a portrait of Ed Bagley Jr. in the office. That's got to be good for something. Farther along the highway, you'll find one motel run by folks with a sense of humor: The Generic Motel. Richly deserving its name, the Generic nonetheless deserves a quick stop. How odd that in a nation of starlights, wigwams, and sunsets, it's the most banal name that seems easiest to recall. Don't be surprised to find yourself jockeying with photographers snapping a kooky shot for their vacation travelogue.

Past Sidney, you'll begin to notice that Nebraska offers more patience for its motel relics than most other states. Not reverence, but a willingness to let old buildings stand. In Lodge Pole, the faded office hints at a decades-old sign for "cabins" while the ruin in Chappell presents a 1930s-era pueblo-revival structure whose crisp white facade glows ethereally against a sharp blue sky. Cruise into Ogallala and check out the Plaza Inn (once known as the Welch Motel). You'll find another midwestern version of streamline-moderne — brick, of

course — with ninety-degree curves and porthole windows. Sadly, the old garages have been transformed into new rooms.

Once you pass through North Platte, you'll want to hit the brakes for the Western Motel, the one with the green and yellow sign and bronking buckaroo. Pretty soon, however, you'll decide it's best not to stick around for long. Head for the Cedar Lodge Motel just down the road. Here in a quiet U-shaped courtyard, birds hop on the lawn and an aging wooden wagon offers sweet reminiscence of the frontier.

Ultimately, your journey may wind up in Grand Island, a quizzical name for flat farmland. Locals explain that a great inland sea once covered this entire region, leaving only the land where the town now lies

breaking the surface. Cruising the surface streets, you'll find all manner of scruffy courts, but hold out for the family-run Lazy V on the east side of town. When twilight descends and the moon begins to rise, you'll find a jubilantly tacky motel sign and a temporary neighborhood of bikers, family trucksters, and long-term locals. Friendly and safe, the Lazy V is easily one of the nicest motels in Nebraska.

CAMPBELL **(AAA)** COURT, NORTH PLATTE, NEBR.

NEVADA

Nevada has lately suffered an identity crisis. In its efforts to curtail recent attempts to fashion itself as a family destination, the Silver State has begun to rediscover its sleazy roots. Of course, the motels of Nevada's prime tourist stops never forgot, offering stained sheets and moaning walls to folks who'd bet their last chip or those who couldn't afford the extravagant rates of the theme-world megaliths that upset the balance sheets of accountants worldwide. With few exceptions like the gruff but sincere Sandman Motel on Reno's faded Fourth Street, Nevada's large city motels are best recalled through decades-old postcards. Best to visit the smaller towns that hang off the interstate like overripe fruit ready to fall.

First stop: Fallon, where an animated cowboy swinging his lariat around the motel moniker offers the quintessential neon experience. Graced with red and blue stripes that line the U-shaped motel, the Lariat reflects the dream and tenacity of its owner, Albert Mustaikis, who has maintained this gem since the years when Lucy and Desi offered first-run entertainment.

In Winnemucca (where peacefully marauding motorcyclists celebrate the so-called runamucca), the Scott Shady Court Motel presents a quiet refuge from the rowdy main drag. Abandoning the dairy business, the Scott family turned to motelling in 1928, enduring the many ups and downs of an economy centered around mining.

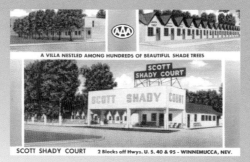

A VILLA NESTLED AMONG HUNDREDS OF BEAUTIFUL SHADE TREES

SCOTT SHADY COURT   2 Blocks off Hwys. U. S. 40 & 95 - WINNEMUCCA, NEV.

To be sure, the Court began humbly. In a history of the motel, Donald H. Erskine quotes one family member's description of the original cabins: "four walls, one door, two windows, a roof and a floor."

Later on when you have returned to the interstate, slow down just before Elko, lower the windows to feel the breeze, and stop at last. Stepping onto the business route, you may hear dogs bark from behind closed screen doors while gray clouds billow overhead. For a time, you may stand in the middle of the street with no traffic while looking down the road into town, unsure of what to expect. Stick around. By the time evening falls, Elko's main street scintillates in flashing, gaudy motel signs that offer more honest thrills than found in the monstrous thoroughfares of Vegas and Reno. The Travelers Motel, the Holiday Motel, the Manor Motor Lodge, and the Centre Motel glow with some of the best neon and friendliest folks.

Finally, make sure you budget time to stay a spell in the town of Wells where rain-slicked tires careen down the highway. Visiting the Lone Star Motel, you may recall the 2001 film, *Joy Ride*. A low budget thriller set along the surreal nightscape of highway diners, convenience stores, and motels, *Joy Ride* introduces a villainous trucker who sets upon two hapless twenty-

somethings, messing with their CB Radio ("it's like a prehistoric internet!"). One dude disguises his voice as a hip roadside chick looking for action. Pretty soon, the clueless roadies learn that they've messed with the wrong trucker. Recalling his mocking growl, "Candy Cane . . . ," you can't help but imagine that this motel would have provided a perfect scene for the film's explosive climax, until you discover that it did.

NEW HAMPSHIRE

When entering the industrial environs of Manchester, a common first stop for folks flying into the Granite State, you may get the wrong idea about New Hampshire. No, the entire state does not sleep until awakened every four years by the hot-air kiss of presidential candidates in power ties and walking shoes. It further turns that out that **New Hampshire** is much more lush and verdant than its southern cities would suggest. Also, with a little searching, you can find some of the nicest motel courts in the Northeast. Along the coast on Route 1,

you might look in vain for the old Sleepy Hollow Motel in Rye that lives on in the form of a postcard depicting a yellow, tail-finned car and friendly green roofs. The old postcard tells the tale of tired motorists who arrived too late to find a room, concluding that the owner phoned to find lodgings for the tourists four miles up the road. Even though you'll drive a long distance to find such hospitality today, don't leave too quickly before checking out a classic local diner. As you'll find throughout the New England states, New Hampshire has some of the finest greasy spoons and all-night coffee joints in the country. Eventually, though, you'll head north to the White Mountains where a set of terrific lodges await.

Along U.S. 2 in Gorham, Bruno and Mary Anne Janicki maintain the Colonial Comfort Inn as well as a hostel for hikers tackling the Appalachian Trail. Recognized as "trail angels" for their dedication to the safety of the AT community, the Janikis have been known to rescue exhausted hikers who overestimated their skills on the 2,100-mile footpath or underestimated the changing climactic conditions that can transform a leisurely stroll into a mortal struggle. When folks finally reach the Janikis's inn, either on foot or by a less strenuous mode of transportation, they find a friendly white chocolate house with

The Sleepy Hollow Motel

U.S. Route #1, Rye N.H.

a diner in front that serves fairly awesome breakfasts. Before you leave, take a look at the newly named Royalty Inn. Once, in the age of linen postcards that advertised private showers and steam heat, the Inn was called the Tourist Village Motel. Now, the place is almost unrecognizable from its earlier days.

A little south where Routes 3 and 302 converge, the Seven Dwarfs Motel advertises itself as a little bit of Switzerland in America, but you'll find yourself close to plenty of pop culture manifestations such as nearby Santa's Village that offers a Yule Log waterslide and Story Land amusement park celebrating its fiftieth year in 2004. However, your best bet lies north near Whitefield at the Mirror Lake Motel. Even though dandelions grow tall along the shuffleboard court, the motel rents clean and comfortable rooms for a surprisingly reasonable rate. Walking toward the lake where guests cast their lines, you may notice the letters M and L on the shutters. Ask the owner what they stand for and she'll simply chuckle and point at the lake.

TOURIST VILLAGE MOTEL
GORHAM, NEW HAMPSHIRE

NEW JERSEY

Let us dispense with niceties and simply state that driving the **New Jersey** turnpike offers you one of the more hellacious auto experiences you're likely to have on the highway. An interminable expanse of stop-and-go traffic, endless construction delays, bizarre turn-offs — added to the fact that you are paying for the privilege — will drive even the most seasoned motorists a bit nuts. You might be tempted to try U.S. 1 or 9, but don't chance them; the old numbered highways now serve as dense parking lots.

Yet, when it seems that you've had just about enough of New Jersey, you stumble onto the Moon Motel in Howell. Rumor has it that the Moon borrowed its theme from a nearby amusement park. Today, you'll find little space age wonder left. Even so, the glowing rockets, plastic satellite, and ringed earth provide a stunning example of motel signage that may easily be classed among the top ten in the nation. Just don't plan on staying overnight.

You know where you're headed: straight down south toward the sea to the place where postwar optimism went after it died pretty much everywhere else. You're going to Wildwood. The atomic starbursts, the neon amoebas, the acres of plate glass, the buildings that appear to be hoisted into the air by sheer optimism alone all find their way to this stretch of amusements and pricey lodges by the beach. Wafting through the salt air, the smell of hot dogs and cotton candy resonates with the memories of summer evenings and carnival games. Best of all, the architecture of Wildwood motels scream of the "not too distant future" as imagined by car commercials that aired in the 1950s.

If you can afford it, you should aim for the heart of the dream: The Starlux boutique motel. There, folks have placed lava lamps in the rooms, begun to rent out Airstream

trailers, and opened an all-glass lounge filled with books about googie, populux, doo-wop, and every other variation of Wildwood design. You'll pay dearly, but you'll not soon forget the glorious neon, the crazy clash of colors, and the friendly staff. One day at least park your clunker at the Starlux and pretend you're driving a caddy with the top down.

The problem is that most Wildwood motels are priced out of reach for the average family driving across country — especially during the summer. But it's certainly worth a couple of hours up and down the main drags. Along with the signs, motels around here attract customers through an astute use of color and shadow; the facades are lit in all hues of orange, pink, green, and purple. Of course, the plastic palm trees are a nice touch, too! It appears that the best way to enjoy a neon tour of Wildwood's wonderful motels is to head south on Atlantic Avenue just after dusk. Most of the signs face that way. But, if your budget is tight, plan to sleep farther inland — perhaps in Rio Grande. But don't be surprised if you find yourself heading back to Wildwood one day, ready to empty your wallet to live in the collective fantasy of the 1950s and 1960s.

NEW MEXICO

New Mexico exceeds your Western fantasies of golden-topped mesas and impossibly tacky turquoise everything. You'll also find some of the grandest old Mom and Pop motels anywhere in the country. Best begin about halfway between Oklahoma City and Albuquerque in Tucumcari — one of those rare towns where the motel lights make you want to get out of the car and walk a while. The strip through town that used to be marked Route 66 is a delight of blinking, glowing, moving color. Classic motels reside along the Mother Road, but there's only one place to stay: The Blue Swallow Motel.

For 40 years, the Blue Swallow was managed by Lillian Redman who arrived in New Mexico by way of a covered wagon in 1916, worked as a Fred Harvey Girl in her youth, and received the Blue Swallow as an engagement present in 1958. In a conversation before her death in 1999, she recalled when the highway was paved with cinders because of its proximity to the railroad and expounded upon her belief that we are all travelers in some way. Even into her nineties, she offered a clean room, hardwood floor, and black and white television to road-weary travelers for eleven bucks and change. Today, Dale and Hilda Bakke own the Blue Swallow Motel, and they're working to update the old court with new telecommunication, color television sets, and (regrettably) somewhat higher prices. The floors are now carpeted and

the walls are freshly painted, but the overall attitude remains the same. Sure, as Hilda remarks, some folks may quibble over the enhancements: "You should have left the old black and white TVs, you should have left the old stuff." Of course, she adds, "we could have left the old creaky mattresses, too."

Sleep in the next morning and plan a leisurely drive to Albuquerque, home of one of a classic stretch of animated neon — ranking up there with Manitou Springs, Colorado, and Wildwood, New Jersey. Grab a room at the El Vado with its pueblo revival architecture and an owner who loves the old highway. Be sure to snap a few shots of the most photogenic motel sign in this part of the country. Of course, the next morning, you'll learn that neon alone is not essential for a great stop when you pull into the Aztec, the oldest motel in the Duke City since its incarnation in 1931 as the Aztec Autocourt.

Spend some time with Mohamed Natha, the owner, and Phyllis Evans, artist-in-residence. Touring the Aztec, you'll find a cross-cultural mélange of broken pottery, old coins, and disparate figurines – all ordered in a manner too artistic to be random, too creative to be mass produced. Not quite an impromptu monument, not quite a love story, this motel is a collaborative exhibition of a mature friendship between two old souls who are determined to create art wherever they find it. Phyllis turns out to be a retired Michigan State University professor of social work who moved to the Aztec temporarily, then never quite left. Since then, she has gathered inspiration from her time in southern Italy to transform the motel into a renaissance experience.

green sunsets. Visiting the Adirondacks in the fall, you'll almost forget the miles of traffic and highway construction you had to endure to get here.

South of Syracuse along Highway 11 in a town called Nedrow, slow down when you spy the pink and green Al-Bel Motel. Since 1956, Alex Johnson's family has tended to their motel as the road convulsed with more cars, businesses, and distractions. Behind a wooden fence, Alex's grandson has planted a tiny grove of apple, pear, and cherry trees. His contribution deserves particular merit when you consider the purposeful obsolescence of motel design, structures built to be quickly torn down should land values change. You know when a family takes the time to plant fruit trees at their motel, chances are they take the time to ensure that their rooms are clean.

If you plan to visit **New York** City, don't imagine you'll simply drop by the first motel you find. Like a military campaign, a visit to the Big Apple requires planning and patience. If you seek more serendipitous lodgings, better head north, past Albany and into the Adirondack Mountains in search of the town of Inlet. Greeting campers, hikers, and fishing buffs, Ken and Linda Nelson's Cottages offer tiny cabins named after New England states, perfectly placed to watch for bears and deer. And, yes, you'll find those oddly shaped chairs whose backs appear like

Farther south, where Highways 20 and 11 cross, an aging relic sign for the Sturdy Maples Motel stands amidst the trees and junk left by passing cars. You'll strain to see the ancient cabins covered in vines in the backyards of recently built homes that align the road. When you encounter a sojourner from the past such as this one, bulbs smashed long ago and wires hanging with no illusion that they may ever be repaired, you might contemplate the changing nature of signs. Once a signal for

a quick night of slumber, maybe to be left in the rearview window the next morning, the marquee now points to decades of motorists and the ever-changing complexion of the roadside.

Eventually, you will visit Niagara Falls, if only because you must. Sadly, the Falls pour forth an ancient torrent of roadside hucksterism and the disappointing reality that even tourist attractions contain sizable zones of blight and despair. The tumbling waters themselves, a magnet for bridal couples without a sense of irony, demand a few moments of your time, providing a contest between yourself and city planners to avoid exorbitant parking fees. Before long, though, you will add to the cacophony of brake lights and car horns on Highway 62, a varied row of fleabag and fairly nice motels. Twilight brings a small number of signs to life, most notably at the

3 Star, Bel-Aire, and the Moonlite Motel. For the night, however, you might best journey east toward the tiny hamlet of Clarence. Stop in the court by the same name and listen to the nighttime symphony of crickets and the occasional passing car. The price is right and the manager doesn't mind if you show up after bedtime.

NORTH CAROLINA

Dappled light drips through sheltering pine trees at the Log Cabin Motor Court, a **North Carolina** stop so lovely that you might not recognize its infamous filmic past. A setting for the 1958 Robert Mitchum film, *Thunder Road*, the Log Cabin Court served as a backdrop for the gritty tale of fast cars and moonshine. Today, NASCAR enthusiasts journey to the site on a peculiar pilgrimage when they stop by Asheville, the birthplace of the sport. Visiting the Log Cabin, many folks stay in the same cabins as their grandparents did before the Interstate Age when the Foster family built these cabins in the authentic style of the region. A well-worn guest register includes a note from one couple that has visited each year on their anniversary for an entire generation. Despite the Court's age — the cabins have stood since the late 1920s — their new owners have managed to provide one modern update to this beloved attraction. While you will not find a phone in any of the eighteen cabins, you will find wireless internet access throughout the property.

Heading west, you'll pass through Maggie Valley, a tourist site that maintains a delicate balance between quaint and tacky. A way-station for hikers and campers tackling the Great Smoky Mountains, the Valley offers more than a dozen pleasant Mom and Pops that advertise creek-side break-

fasts and evening marshmallow roasts. Most are reasonably priced and nicely appointed. Of course, you cannot go wrong with the Holiday Motel with its red rocking chairs, wagon wheels, and horseshoes. While the cars stream past, some filled with restless kids and road-weary parents, savor the moment of calm and contemplate, perhaps, a dip in the pool.

If, however, you continue along the windy road toward Cherokee, you'll encounter a truly gorgeous neon sign. The Pink Motel

stands along the banks of the Oconaluftee River in mute resistance to time and copyright laws. It may take a while, but the lithe pixie casts a spell on motorists who pass by, reminding you of a signature product of a certain amusement park conglomerate. If you hold out until twilight, you are rewarded when the motel's real magic emerges. As the clouds glow a milky pink and purple, the neon fairy comes alive and reveals a sublime vision sure to delight

ASHEVILLE, NORTH CAROLINA

THE **Log Cabin** MOTOR **Court**

(Circa 1930)

even the most hardened motorist — or entertainment lawyer.

Just south of the Virginia border, the town of Mount Airy may look familiar to lovers of old time television searching for small town Americana. Mount Airy provided the backdrop for Andy Griffith's imaginary town of Mayberry and continues to offer architectural props for modern sojourns to simpler times. Check out the colonial-style Mayberry Motor Inn along the U.S. 52 bypass. It's the one with "Sheriff Taylor's" squad car and a truck from "Emmet's Fix-it-Shop" parked in front. Of course, fans of the old Holiday Inn "Great Sign" will also delight to discover one of the few of these marvels still standing just down the road. Repainted as the Star Light Motel, the sign offers a striking reminder of The Nation's Innkeeper before it became yet another monopoly piece for an international conglomerate.

NORTH DAKOTA

Like Rodney Dangerfield, **North Dakota** seems to get no respect. Its neighbor to the south has those huge concrete heads, Montana to the west has a distinquished nickname (Big Sky Country), and Minnesota earns admiration for its thousands of lakes. North Dakota brings to mind, well, nothing in particular. Don't miss out, though. The Peace Garden State (so named for its role in helping the United States and Canada maintain the longest undefended national border in the world) offers vistas of gorgeous scenery, a surprisingly large degree of verdant green plains, and a state full of friendly straight-shooting folks. Best of all, along the empty stretches of road that crisscross the state, you might even put the pedal down a bit (within reason and common sense, of course).

Entering the state, you might as well check out Fargo. The city won't remind you of

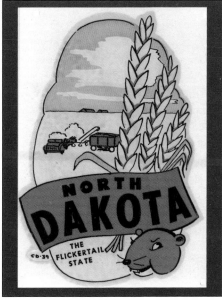

the clever film of the same name unless you visit in the depths of the state's icebox winter. But west of town on Highway 10, you'll fall for the mellow vibe at the Sunset Inn where beautiful carnations grow adjacent to the road. Offering a game room, indoor pool, and waterslide, the Sunset is also home to concrete deer grazing on the leaves. Owned by the same family for two decades, the Sunset reflects a Mom and Pop mentality that only looks like a pricey hotel. Nearby, a genuine meat-eater's paradise can be found. Smoky's Tavern and Steakhouse (with none of the artificial stimulants that cause blackening, which have spawned a thousand Texas-style pre-fabs).

Roll into the somewhat scruffy outskirts of Bismarck by twilight and catch the Motor Hotel — it's the one using the town's name to grab your attention. Glowing pink and green, the Bismarck Motor Hotel has a sign that offers passing resemblance to one of those Holiday Inn "Great Signs," including a glowing star atop a funky-shaped facade, but no one will confuse the rooms for the "Host From Coast to Coast." Chat up the local kids riding bikes up and down the road and they'll give you their best estimates on where else you might stay nearby. The bottom line: the town's neon is pretty good but you ought to keep moving.

If you can keep your eyes open, reach for the western edge of the state, heading for Dickinson. There, the Nodak Motel presents itself in garish pink neon strips that are best discovered when sprinkles of rain have begun to obscure your vision. As the weight of your drive bares down upon you, pull in and chat with the motel's owner, Scott Martin. You'll also find refurbished rooms at reasonable prices. Best of all, you're perfectly positioned to shoot southward to Regent along the Enchanted Highway, a fantasy land of giant locusts, an oversized Teddy Roosevelt, and real roadside pheasants that practically shout in a New York accent to cars racing by, "Hey, I'm walking here!" Before you leave North Dakota, swing south to Bowman in search of the Trail Motel. Red and yellow plastic balls sit atop the otherwise unremarkable sign. However, the marquee reminds you of the no-nonsense character of the folks who eke out a living in the Rodney Dangerfield of states. The sign simply says, "Stay."

OHIO

Ohio offers plenty of classic motels along the old numbered highways that crisscross the Buckeye State. In fact, the authors of this book spent four years cruising its back roads in search of neon before we settled in California. Upon our return, we found that Ohio, like so many states, has lost many of its original motels as streets were widened and standards were raised. How sad that so many have been run too far down and eventually demolished. Of course, when describing the former Bambi Motel in Columbus, Stephen Lemons writes in *Salon Magazine* how many slipped into a parallel universe most easily visualized in David Lynch films like *Blue Velvet* and *Wild at Heart*: "a realm of half-full ashtrays, shot glasses brimming with bourbon and dames in horn-rims and bullet bras."

And then there's the 40 Motel in Columbus. Like many classic motels, the National Road aligned 40 Motel maintains its grand sign — the largest neon sign in the city — through the wonder of grandfathering. Local brahmins may complain, but the swooping arrow that practically sucks tired drivers off the highway stays year after year. Best of all, the 40 continues to attract motorists with its quirky marquee quotes. Examples: "Why is the alphabet in that order? Is it because of that song?," "If the number 2 pencil is so popular, why is it number 2?," and "Don't sweat petty things and don't pet sweaty things."

DAYTON

VICTORY MOTOR COURT FRANKLIN

ROUTE 25

CINCINNATI

OHIO'S FINEST

Victory Motor Court

Modern, Steam Heat, Private Baths

ON ROUTE 25   FRANKLIN, OHIO

15 Miles South of Dayton
30 Miles North of Cincinnati
PHONE 719

R. S. FAUST
RES. PH. 384-12

W. H. ZIMMERMAN
RES. PH. 384-W1

Baker's Motel

The motel itself occupies a tenuous position along an increasingly urban maze of fast food joints and past-midnight businesses. Step through the lobby though and you'll meet fine folks all too willing to point out speed traps and suggest a good place to grab a bite.

If you make it down to Athens, check out the Sunset Motel. Surrounded by forest-covered hills, the motel's sign offers an awesome welcome to road travelers with its swooping arrow and bold red neon (when it works). As twilight falls, crickets chirp and cars rumble by. The occupied rooms glow green through drawn blinds. You may not be able to tell from outside, but the Sunset has existed in many incarnations, dating back to the late 19th century when it was a five bedroom lodging house. Today, like many college-town motels, the Sunset survives with the help of visiting parents and adventuresome students.

Finally, if your journey takes you north along Highway 20, say hello to Sara and Steve Whitman who work hard to keep the neon humming at the Old Orchard Motel in Fremont. Here, you encounter another criterion for selecting a great motel: if the owners live in a house on the property, you can rest assured that they invest more than mere money to keep the place running. Even with the Ohio Turnpike zipping

motorists across the northern tier of the Buckeye State, the old U.S. highway that runs parallel manages to deposit enough folks in Fremont to keep the lights on. Sara laughs when she recalls how her motel put two kids through college and keeps the family out of debt. Thinking ahead to their eventual retirement, Sara contemplates how they will pass their motel to another family one day, help them make the down payment, and keep the business in good hands.

OKLAHOMA

Route 66 cruises through **Oklahoma**, passing relics in Afton like the oft-photographed Rest Haven Motel before setting its course toward Tulsa. You wouldn't guess by the interstates that cleave through the city, but Tulsa earns its "Green Country" nickname thanks to an impressive number of parks and gardens. The city also boasts an international-caliber collection of art deco buildings from the 1930s and 1940s. An essential stop on your journey is the Desert Hills Motel. While you may think more of oil derricks dotting the landscape, this motel harkens to an older myth of the frontier in the form of a glowing neon cactus that waits for the silky sky to melt into night. Nearby, you'll find the Oasis Motel whose pastel tubes and glowing moon stand out against the boring roadside clutter.

Continuing toward Oklahoma City, pull into Chandler ("Pecan capital of the

World") and visit the Lincoln Motel. There, you will encounter two rows of red wooden cabins with green benches and an American flag that snaps in the breeze. Maintained since 1939, the Lincoln just might be the nicest motel in the Sooner State. Eventually, though, you'll continue west toward OK-City. With the exception of 66 Bowl, the town and its outlying areas have largely abandoned the Mother Road, even while the ghosts of the past reside on the walls of old buildings.

Even today, the neighboring community of Yukon advertises "No finer or more modern mills in America!" on its towering grain elevator. But the classic Yukon Motel sign, once towering with bouncy red squares, has been recently replaced with a standard-issue backlit plastic box. Stay on Route 66 toward Elk City in search of the Big 8 Motel with its swooping yellow arrow and turquoise banner advertising "Amarillo's Finest" (for its placement in the film *Rain Man*), and you'll be disappointed once more. The motel has forsaken its past to become another dusty pit stop.

Keep driving toward Texas and the flat expanse of the open range. You're heading for Sayre and the Western Motel. A few years back, we asked the owner about this gorgeous sign, complete with cactus and desert sands. He answered, "About ten cars

a day come by here to take pictures of that sign — especially since all the European magazines show it. Folks gotta take a picture to prove they were there."

Heading north toward Kansas, stop in Enid where you can't miss the deep purple hue of the Lazy H Motel where fat, content goldfish swim lazy circles in the lobby tank. Arun and his brother Pete were electrical and mechanical engineers in India before switching careers four years ago. When they arrived, the Lazy H was pretty banged up. Since then, the brothers repainted the walls, renovated the fixtures, refurbished the lobby, and installed a koi pond outside. Like many members of their community, virtually everyone in the brothers' extended family helps run the motel, proving that the Lazy H deserves a name change.

OREGON

Entering **Oregon** from the east along the famed trail that brought immigrants to the Beaver State, you may find yourself drawn to Baker City, the so-called Queen of the Inland Empire. Nearby Hells Canyon with its petroglyphs and challenging hikes may wear you out, but you'll rest easy at the Oregon Trail Motel. A local artisan has crafted a few quirky pieces on the property and the glow of the friendly office looks pretty inviting after you've spent an hour careening through the mountains bordering Idaho. Later in the evening, drift into town to check out the deco features of the

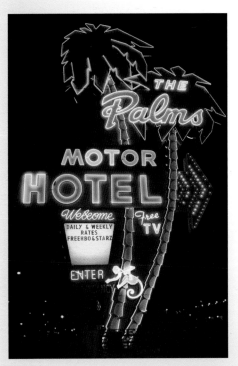

neon Eltrym Theater. As the cool breeze raises a few goose bumps, try to make sense of the quizzical name. If you ask, they'll tell you about the original owner's wife, Myrtle, who refused to allow a movie house to be named after her. Suddenly you'll understand how Myrtle's husband got the last laugh.

Drive parallel to the Columbia River as it seeks the ocean and you'll find yourself in Portland whose alignment with Highway 99 provides an impressive array of neon dreams to photograph, notably the Capitol Hill Motel. By day, you'll find a sullen display of red brick and shingles. But the night brings another side of the old motel in gas-lit yellow, orange, and green. Sadly, plenty of other Portland beauties have lost their battles with history or remain and continue their struggle with illegal goings-on. Your best bet when you visit the City of Roses is to seek out the Palms Motor Hotel, the one whose glowing sign features tall electric trees, free TV, and a neon monkey. Some folks report a remarkable similarity between this motel and the Desert Palms Motel in Kent Anderson's violent depiction of mid-1970s Portland in *Night Dogs*. But don't let that turn you off. The motel has recently undergone refurbishment and the rates are reasonable. Best of all, if you simply cannot get enough of a tiki fix from the Palms Motel, check out

the nearby Alabi Lounge for a strong and syrupy Mai Tai.

Finally, we'll cheat a bit and highlight a southern Oregon treasure that's not quite a motel but will provide an unforgettable night, nonetheless. Michael Garnier's Out 'n' About Treesort in Takilma offers a forest of rooms perched in fourteen treehouses, a couple that even offer bathroom facilities among the branches. More than a quirky night's stay (plan for a minimum two or three nights in summer months), the Treesort also includes an institute where folks gather to discuss treehouse design and its correlation to the unique spirituality that comes from a genuine love of the Siskiyou Forest. Best of all, each guest is entitled to an unlimited supply of Fantasy Flakes for breakfast, the "ethereal serial" that harkens back to Michael's counter-culture roots. Sure we mentioned this unique lodge in a previous book, *Road Trip America*, but come on: in this volume that celebrates offbeat lodgings, we're not going to forget to showcase an opportunity for you to sleep in a tree!

PENNSYLVANIA

The Lincoln Highway stretches through **Pennsylvania** along the road that would become U.S. Highway 30. Decades after the modern turnpike bypassed the famed tourist road, you can still find old and new road signs painted red, white, and blue that feature a bronze colored bust of Abraham Lincoln — and dozens of gas stations, diners, and motels that evoke the Lincoln image. Perhaps the most beloved of the bunch is the Lincoln Motor Court located about five miles West of Bedford. A U-shaped gathering of individual cabins built in the 1940s, the Court earns its reputation for friendliness and cleanliness thanks to the twenty-year efforts of Deb and Bob Altizer who maintain their sixty-year-old units with every country amenity and not a phone in sight. Deb explains, "I try to keep the rooms like my grandmother's farm house . . . and you can walk into a room, sit on the bed, and imagine your grandparents on their honeymoon."

Heading east toward Lancaster, you might drop by the Red Caboose Motel where you can sleep in a twenty-five-ton train. With little prodding, the owners of the Red Caboose will tell you about the motel's founder, Donald M. Denlinger, who took a dare to bid on a dingy collection of rusty hulks, never expecting he'd come to own a small fleet of trains. Imagine his surprise when he received a snippy phone call demanding he take possession of the locomotives immediately. Demonstrating the spirit of ingenuity that often accompanies desperation, Denlinger found some land

Hood's Tavern & Tourist Court

Phone IMPERIAL 300. On U. S. 30 and 22. 11 Miles West of Pittsburgh, Pa. R. D. No. 1 Oakdale, Pa.

and arranged the trains into a motel. Boasting an on-site restaurant and all manner of tourist activities like a petting zoo, the Red Caboose has provided one of America's most unique accommodations since opening in 1970.

However, like a page from a Choose Your Own Adventure book, you might just as easily depart Highway 30 in search of Shartlesville. There, you may be discouraged at the new name of the former Fort Motel; it's now the Budget Inn. However, the ranch-style motel maintains its independence, purchasing the name only to deliver more customers. As it has for years, the motel offers a nifty set of theme rooms — dozens of them — including the starlight room, the millionaire room, and heaven and hell. Near the former Fort Motel, you'll find Roadside America, one

Come to PENNSYLVANIA

PENNSYLVANIA'S GRAND CANYON
WELLSBORO, PA.
ROOSEVELT HIGHWAY   U. S. ROUTE 6

of the coolest and tackiest highway attractions ever built, renowned for its massive collection of miniature towns and communities selected from around the country.

From Shartlesville, you could head northward in search of the Blue Ridge Motel in New Milford. The old-school sign, a giant marquee held aloft by twin poles, rusts forlornly as evening falls and car lights pass by. A storm blew the neon away a while back, but the new owners demonstrate the triumph of hope over experience as they plan to refurbish their damaged sign when the budget allows. A mere mile away, the interstate carves through the countryside. But here, when the morning mist hushes the noise and reveals the chattering of crickets, you're right where you ought to be.

RHODE ISLAND

Rhode Island presents an impressive amount of coastline and gorgeous scenery for a state barely fifty miles wide. And along its torturously complicated southern border, U.S. 1 snakes its way south from Providence to Pawcatuck. The old numbered highway offers a clear choice to tourists who'd just as soon see the Ocean State as merely pass through it on Interstate 95. But even Highway 1 rolls through a bit too easily. If you want to drop into the tiny towns dotting the coastline, you must detour southward along local roads that call for a gentle touch on the accelerator. The rewards for these excursions merit the risks. You may end up staying in Rhode Island far longer than you'd planned.

When passing through Providence, a town that resembles Cleveland in its decaying architecture and ill-fated attempt at urban renewal, check out the funky boutiques and restaurants that have begun to take root, but remember that the richest line of Mom and Pop motels awaits visitors to the southern coast between Charlestown and the Connecticut border. In Charlestown, Phil and Ann's Sunset Motel invites guests to a quiet U-shaped stop near the beach with some fairly impressive fishing, if striped bass and flounder are your thing. The wood-paneled rooms are clean and reasonably priced and the owners are friendly. But if you drive 3,000 miles to meet Phil and Ann, you'll be disappointed. The current owners are Gil and Maureen Barnes.

Head west past Dunns Corners and you'll discover a building that resembles a Swiss chalet: The Cornerstone Inn. In the lobby, you'll find local crafts for sale and a brief refuge from the chillingly bizarre Dusty's Snowman statue next door that, Janus-like, gazes down both directions of the road. Nearby on the Old Post Road, the Blue Star Motor Inn awaits. When you're on the road long enough, dodging backlit plastic marquees that hardly apologize for their lame replacement of the signs that once stood in their places, you get nervous when a motel named Blue Star announces itself

down the road. These days you can be certain you will not see a Blue Star, merely a san serif lettered box that conjures up nothing but the depressing choice to stay in yet another forgettable motel. But when you cruise toward Westerly, you'll fall under the spell of a genuine Blue Star standing atop a tall pole. At last, a real motel with a pool, picnic grounds, and rooms still advertising wall-to-wall carpeting as a selling point.

One thing to remember when visiting Rhode Island — and this advice doesn't even contemplate a stay near the yacht clubs and polo grounds of Newport: summer travelers are bound to get gouged with multiple-day requirements and beach

prices even when staying blocks away from the surf. Put simply, the Ocean State will take a chunk out of the wallet of any travelers who fail to call ahead and bargain for the lowest rate they can swing.

SOUTH CAROLINA

South Carolina represents more than the threat of crafty cops in aviator glasses awaiting the next lead-footed out-of-towner. But, when it comes to motels, not much more. If you find yourself in the capital city of Columbia at the Grand Motel, don't let the fact that the office sells condoms (a buck a piece seems to be a going rate) dissuade you from chatting a bit. At night, the sign glows with a pulsating green star that throbs to a jaunty mechanical rhythm. At one time, the owners took a look at the cost of repairing the lights and gave up, planning to tear the sign down, but a local preservation group petitioned for history's sake to keep the motel's peculiar neon beauty alight. So the tubes were repaired and the star lit once more. You might drop by and thank them, even if you're just passing through.

Heading east toward Myrtle Beach, land of a thousand miniature golf courses, you might enjoy a popular Bible Belt road trip game: comparing the gifts of wit and whimsy to be found on church marquees. South Carolinians seem to draw particular pleasure in the pursuit of the perfect adage. Some of the best along these roads read, "Bibles that are falling apart usually belong to people who are not," and, "God answers knee mail." Snacking on some boiled peanuts (a southern delicacy whose rapture eludes most city folk), press onward until you see the shore. See if you'll find motel names like the Cin-D-Ann Motel, Rockin K Motel, and the Tricia-Lyn Resort Motel anywhere else but in South Carolina.

Still, you know that you cannot leave South Carolina without a night with Pedro. Under tussled sheets with the hint of tequila on his breath, he waits for you in the tackiest motel in America: South of the Border. From the hundreds of miles of day-glo billboards that entice motorists

with god-awful puns ("you never sausage a place") to the giant neon caricature of Pedro, so offensive that the Mexican embassy once complained, South of the Border has grown much since its 1949 beginnings as a beer stand. Featuring 300 rooms, "heir conditioned" honeymoon suites, and a sombrero-shaped restaurant, SOB (yep, that's what locals call it) absolutely will draw you into its quirky orbit.

Stay the night, but don't forget to drive farther south through the town of Dillon and visit the wrecks of abandoned motor courts that were wiped from existence after SOB

began to grow and mutate. Keep driving; you won't get lost. Pedro glows just over the horizon. It's easy to hate this mad counterfeit Tijuana that casts such a long shadow over the highway. But, like the real Tijuana south of the real border, you have to visit at least once. Stumble in awe under the glaring lights, stand in the pedestrian walkway — staring down the lumbering trucks — and take a picture next to Pedro like so many have before. You can't help yourself, and you'll probably return. South of the Border, like a stinky cigar, is a guilty pleasure impossible to ignore.

South Dakota deserves more attention than it gets from the passing parade of high school busses dutifully making the trek to Mount Rushmore. Sure, you have to go eventually, see the film, buy the miniature, and take the picture. But remember that the state also offers a fascinating array of tacky tourist traps and unforgettable scenery, not to mention some truly memorable motels.

One way to get started is to visit Belle Fourche on the west side of the state. There, you'll find the Weyer Motel and Jewelry Store, a pretty rare combination when you think about it. Each of the motel's eleven rooms are surfaced with a kind of rock facade that creates the illusion that the place grew from some volcanic eruption. Don't be fooled, though. The rooms are clean and neat thanks to Deloris Weyer who has worked in the motel industry since she was thirteen. One of her family members runs the nearby Reed Motel, built by CC Miller. The separate cabins are nice enough, but the main reason to stop is to seek out CC's name written in shark's teeth in the sidewalk.

Heading for Spearfish just a little south of Belle Fourche? Bring your camera. Practically every outer surface of the All Star Traveler's Inn is covered with murals thanks to an itinerant painter who discov-

KUILMAN'S MOTEL ON HIGHWAY 12, THIRD AVE. EAST, MOBRIDGE, SOUTH DAKOTA, 25 UNITS

KUILMAN'S MOTEL — ON HIGHWAY 10, EAST MAIN AVE. at 20th — BISMARCK, N. D., 23 UNITS

ered a wonderful way to see the country and earn free lodging. Here Peter Teekamp has painted a "History of America," beginning with a Native American myth of the world's founding and ending with the aftermath of the September 11th attacks. You'll admire the artist's ingenuity as he integrates air conditioners and exposed pipes into his artistic vision. As the local paper sums up, "Some people take pictures when they travel, Peter Teekamp leaves pictures behind."

Heading back east toward Rapid City, you'll pass through the remnants of Mom and Pop motels long gone to seed. But make time (lots of it) to drop by the Corral Motel, the one with the bumper sticker in the office that reads, "Charlton Heston is my president." Talk with the owner, a former detective who still claims to maintain files on 65,000 people, and you'll learn more about Indian Satanists, drug-crazed banditos, political scandals, and Chicago gangsters than you ever wanted to know. Or, you can just keep driving toward the town of Wall where the Welsh Motel's green and red color scheme looks like Christmas year round.

Taking a southerly course through South Dakota (stopping at Wall Drug and the Mitchell Corn Palace, naturally), don't forget the town of Murdo and the Sioux

Motel where Bonnie has scoured antique stores for cow skulls and wooden sculptures to attract visitors to her digs. Get back on the road and aim for Sioux Falls and the Cloud 9 Motel. As dusk descends and the pungent odor of the nearby stockyards drifts over the parked semis, take a look back down the road. From Rapid City to the end of the line, you've traveled much more than mere distance.

Tennessee presents its visitors a poignant display of small business hospitality and chain efficiency, illustrating the struggle between the two. Perhaps no better picture of this struggle may be found than in Nashville where the famed Travelers Rest Motel, once noted as "one of the last Mom and Pop motels left," became a parcel of raw land for a national drug store. The building was burned down by the local fire department. Even Nashville's Loveless Motel and Cafe offers merely a reflection of its motel roots in the form of a stunning neon sign that looks like it hasn't been cleaned in years. But the motel was long ago gutted (don't let the lit vacancy sign fool you) and turned into a buffet style diner. The news isn't all bad though. Walk into the stone and wood paneled office building and your mouth will water as the aroma of southern biscuits curls around your nose. The unostentatious structure seems to be held up solely by the support of framed newspaper articles and magazine cover stories on the diner, not to mention the testimonials of folks like Wink Martindale, Dick Van Patten, and Strom Thurmond.

Head north a bit, riding alternate 41 into Clarksville, and try not to slam on the brakes too suddenly when spotting the unmistakable likeness of a Holiday Inn "Great Sign," named for its towering

height, explosion of neon, and pulsating star. Almost impossible to find now, original "Great Signs" represented the vision of Kimmons Wilson whose Holiday Inn chain influenced a generation of motel designers and managers. However, this "great sign" was built by William H. Hall who admired Wilson's business and found a partner who knew the famed hotelier pretty well. In fact, William recalls they were "so tight they squeaked." Problem was, they didn't want to buy the franchise that would have cost ten thousand dollars.

LEAHY'S TOURIST COURT — 3070 SUMMER AVE. — MEMPHIS, TENN.

"So instead of buying the franchise, we just stoled everything we could out of Holiday Inn." In 1953, they built the Vacation Motor Hotel that stands today as a faded memory of a hospitality giant and its impact on the travel industry.

Head West to Memphis, a town that deserves fame and infamy for more than Holiday Inns. Sliding past the theme-park blues ambiance of Beale Street, you encounter an historic remnant in a decaying part of town: the Lorraine Motel, site of Martin Luther King Junior's 1968 assassination. Viewing the horrific photograph of onlookers pointing from a balcony toward the location of the shooting, it's easy to forget that the Civil Rights leader was killed in a fairly ordinary motor court that would be otherwise condemned and forgotten by now. Indeed, the Lorainne faced demolition in the 1980s before a group of historically-minded preservationists rounded up the funds to transform the motel into the National Civil Rights

Museum, an impressive display that reminds visitors of the violence and courage called forth by a nation confronting the sins of its past. While the museum appears to dwarf the tragic climax of King's life, preservationists do history credit by leaving the motel — and the room of his last day — intact.

TENNESSEE

For some road trippers, the first glimpse of the Lone Star State offers little but flat plains and howling winter winds. The 177 miles of desolate expanse stretching between Oklahoma and New Mexico invokes little more than time to contemplate the open road. However, several worthwhile motels reside within the **Texas** panhandle, including one relic that provides an essential stop for lovers of the Mother Road. Under the shadow of a grain elevator, the 66 Courts is located on the outskirts of Groom, near the largest cross in the western hemisphere. This beloved relic offers a photogenic reminder of bygone Mom and Pops bypassed by the interstate highway system.

For a more lively stop, drop by Amarillo and the Big Texan. While plenty of guidebooks rhapsodize about its 72-ounce steak deal (a free meal if you eat the whole thing with all the trimmings within a single hour), you should not bypass the splendid motel. The stage-set facade offers the illusion of an Old West cow town, complete with ersatz Victorian hotels and fake billiard halls. The rooms might be a bit pricey, but you'll hardly find a nicer stay with swinging bathroom doors that look like they were lifted from a western movie.

A more subdued motel opportunity may be found along U.S. 287 in Clarindon. Adding to the list of humble motel names

HELENA COURT
U. S. HIGHWAY 59 - 90 A
75 AND 35
HOUSTON,
TEXAS

HELENA
TOURIST
COURT

Member of
TEXAS MOTOR COURTS
ASSOCIATION

AAA
Approved

UNITED
MOTOR COURTS
For
Surpassed
Comfort

AMERICAN MOTOR
HOTEL ASSOCIATION
AMHA

East Side of City
On New
Super Gulf Freeway 75

Approved By
DUNCAN HINES

use room linen to polish shoes." Lean back and your head bumps against an iron headboard bolted right into the masonry. In the bathroom, there's mint green and Pepto-Bismol pink tile. Stepping into a room at the Coral Motel is like stepping into a partially completed set for a time travel movie in which the details aren't quite right. You've got new carpet and a 1980s touchtone phone competing with 1960s furniture.

Finally, if you happen to amble by the Lone Star State's capital of Austin, you can't miss dropping by the Austin Motel (yes, the one that looks like a giant glowing phallus). The place has got history to burn. Begun in 1938, the motel has weathered the city's changing times — fighting back the influx of economic misery that had decimated much of Austin's former charm until its more recent renaissance. Telling stories of how she learned her trade the hard way, Dottye Dean writes, "All we can do is to make the motel the best that we can make it and live our lives with passion, creativity, and love for our families, our work, our community and our world — so that the years that are gifted to us to live on this sweet little earth will be meaningful and worthwhile."

such as Ho Hum (Reno, Nevada) and Generic (Sidney, Nebraska), you'll find the "It'll Do" Motel. You may wish to stay in the nicer Western Sky, which proclaims "Through these doors pass the most welcomed guests in America." But take at least a moment to pay homage to the honesty of its more forthright cousin down the road.

If you find yourself cruising into the dusty south Texas environs of El Paso, downshift onto Montana Avenue where you'll discover a clutch of solid motels. The nicest of the bunch is the Coral Motel with its black velvet paintings, wooden beam ceilings, and southwestern themed blankets. The owner must like them, posting, "Do not

Today the nicest motel in Salt Lake awaits practically under the silvery spires of the Salt Lake temple, spiritual center of the Latter Day Saints. The City Creek Inn reminds its visitors of Mormon history with its neon depiction of an ox cart hauling a pioneer family across the desert sands, past a glowing green cactus. One evening during our visit, three modern sojourners — elderly ladies who have driven twelve hours straight — show up in search for a room. The only problem is they carry cash and no credit cards. The young woman behind the desk sheepishly admits that she must request a fifty-dollar deposit: "We don't want any partiers here." This is, after all, Salt Lake City. One woman laughs in gentle astonishment. "Well, we were thinking about ordering a pizza. Does that count?"

Beyond the miles of burning salt flats, past the towering mesas and soaring rocks, through the rolling tumbleweeds that hurl themselves in your way, **Utah**'s Salt Lake City waits. Built for no other reason than the faith of Mormon pioneers that this was indeed "the place," Salt Lake reclines in its jagged basin and reflects the interconnected histories of hundreds of tourist court and motor hotel owners who knew that folks needed to stop *somewhere* in the middle of the vast desert. Flip through a pile of old postcards and the forgotten motels arise where supermarkets and gas stations now stand. Once the Casa Blanca Auto Court advertised steam heat, tile baths, and a radio in each room. Nearby, the Mission Motor Lodge, its red tiles and orange-arched garages a Spanish revival fantasy in stucco, was once "new, modern, and carpeted."

Heading southeast toward Heber City, don't be surprised if you think you've passed through an invisible portal to Switzerland. The snow-capped mountains and vibrant lineage of original Swiss immigrants inspired a more recent revival of playful cuckoo clock architecture epitomized by the Swiss Alps Inn. Its second-story tower greets you with a bearded herder, a "Swiss Miss," and rotating mountain goats. The owner explains, "We wanted something that reminded us of *The Sound of Music*." When reminded that the

beloved film was based in Austria, she laughs readily and admits, "It's close enough."

Before leaving the Beehive State, don't forget to visit Green River, site of the friendly Robbers Roost Motel. Drive during the early evening as the moon hangs over the horizon and the setting sun pours out an orangish-red watercolor. Over the horizon along Highway 50, the Robbers Roost Motel emerges with the soft glow of a plastic beauty atop the neon sign. The motel's name may put you off, but remember this region was home to outlaws like Butch Cassidy, the Wild Bunch, and Kid Curry who deposited their loot after robbing banks and stagecoaches. Down the road, the similarly gorgeous Sleepy Hollow Motel entreats visitors with its slogan: "Charming, Cozy, Comfortable, But Never Costly."

UTAH MOTOR PARK — 972 SO. STATE ST. — SALT LAKE CITY, UTAH

Finally, if you're heading east along Highway 40, don't forget to pay homage to Dinah the Dinosaur, the shockingly pink mascot of Vernal whose come-hither lashes have drawn thousands of motorists off the highway for a closer look. Shoot a photo and have a laugh, but remember too that Dinah once graced the entrance of the Motel Dine-A-Ville, a legend that stands now only in memory.

Lynada Motel
2744 Washington Blvd. (U. S. 91-89-30 So.) Ogden, Utah.

Recommended by Duncan Hines in "Lodging for a Night."

VERMONT

Touring the Green Mountain State along U.S. 2, you might head toward Montpelier, easily the nicest state capital city in the nation. Small and friendly, Montpelier reflects **Vermont**'s mellow vibe and Yankee practicality. However, the place to stay lies back east near St. Johnsbury. Driving past, you may spy rows of plastic chairs and a set of quaint yellow and white cabins overlooking Joe's Pond. Beth Perreault and her family maintain the tiny but immaculate Injunjoe Court. They spin tales of the Abernacky Indian who used to guide people through the area. The Court earned its name because, "rumor has it that Injun Joe used to sleep on the hill." Heading past Montpelier (it won't take

long), aim for Burlington on the coast of Lake Champlain.

Once you arrive, drop by the former Motel Brown (now the somewhat more delicate sounding Champlain Inn), and thank the new owners for working hard to return a decrepit rat hole into a hopeful vision of its former self, a lodge once visited by John Kennedy and his 1960 campaign staff. Security has become tight but the rooms are clean once more and long term residents up to no good have left. Managed by a former state trooper, the Champlain Inn deserves a second look by vacationers who had wisely steered clear in the past. For every motel that has fallen on hard times,

it's inspiring to discover that some can return from beyond the brink.

If you find yourself on the southwestern corner of Vermont, drop by Bennington where several nice courts can be found. But if you happen to visit Vermont during the Christmas Holiday season, you might as well stay at a motel that will send you home with a free Vermont tree you select and cut (assuming you don't want one of the pre-cut ones they offer as well). The Fife 'n Drum Motel offers a package deal that includes a local meal, two-night stay in their comfy lodge, and a tree. Ed and Vally McCauley are betting you'll make your stay a holiday tradition.

The most essential motel stop in Vermont, of course, waits in the pleasant town of Fairlee, north of White River Junction along old U.S. 5. The Fairlee Motel and Drive-In has stood for more than five decades. While the sun dips beyond the horizon, local cars and pickups trundle into the grassy plain behind the twelve-unit motel. On a cool summer evening, kids cavort near the snack stand where the odor of food you would only eat in a drive-in wafts under a cloudless sky. The Fairlee plays family-friendly, first-run films, but you won't care what they're showing. The mere fact that you've got a room with the most comfortable view in the house ensures a pretty good show. Like its distant cousin in Monte Vista in Colorado, the Fairlee invites a combo-crowd of folks who love roadside motels and those who crave drive-in theaters. Given that both suffer the ravages of progress, they ought to gather together more often.

The Green
Mountain State

VERMONT

VIRGINIA

Virginia has long attracted highway tourists in search of easily consumed history and genuinely beautiful scenery. The old numbered roads oblige with aging but well maintained tourist courts, particularly along old U.S. 1. However, you should focus your attention on the western tip of Old Dominion. There, the Robert E. Lee Motel decays along U.S. 19 in Hilander Park. The Lee's turquoise sign contains all the components of a streamlined dream, including aero-dynamic tubing and port-holes strategically situated in case the motel should be placed in a wind tunnel. An appropriate station along the pilgrim path of any roadside photographer, the motel no longer offers rooms — just memories.

Continue northward past the Moonlight Drive-In (whose glowing orb and sparkling stars continue to enchant despite the tide of suburban movie google-plexes), and search out the Alpine Inn. The motel's sharp lines and lengthy expanse juts awkwardly from the rolling green hills, but the rooms are clean and the prices are fair. Before cocooning in your room to catch a film or take a nap, check out the tiny cemetery near the property where the stones — some ostentatious, others more humble — commemorate family names dating to the mid-nineteenth century.

Heading toward Shenandoah National Park, you may be tempted to settle for one of the many anonymous chain lodges along the interstate. Instead, stay on U.S. Highway 11 and pull off in the town of New Market where the Blue Ridge Inn awaits. Located on four acres of land that offer a near-perfect view of the Massanutten mountain range, the Inn provides a countrified burst of gingham quilts, sunflower designs, straw hats, and welcome signs. More importantly, the Blue Ridge attends to one detail forgotten by most other budget courts: it provides more pillows than you could ever possibly need. After a dozen hours on the road, you'll delight at that particular problem. The next morning, plop onto one of the comfy chairs next to every door and wait for the

local cat to amble by in search of gentle scratches.

Continuing toward Front Royal, you'll find a hidden nest of valley view cabins, its Motor Court sign lost within an overgrowth of trees. Drive into town, though, for an essential stop for followers of architectural evolution. In his book, *How Buildings Learn*, Stuart Brand described the odd ways in which our environment reflects the changing narratives of our lives as buildings adapt and conform to altering trends and value systems. A perfect exam-

ple of this phenomenon lies on the north side of Front Royal: The Shenandoah Motel, a strange convergence of primitive stone and streamline moderne design. On the other side of rustic cottages, you'll find the trademark boxy style of an architect who'd seen the film *Things to Come* one too many times. Essential motifs of the 1930s, the motel's brick glass and steamship railings evoke an age of confidence in the midst of Depression-age construction.

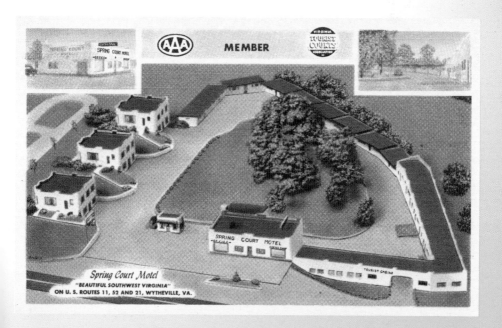

WASHINGTON

Throughout the state of **Washington**, Highway 99 pulsates with neon and aging Mom and Pop businesses along a north-south axis. In Seattle, 99 adopts the name Aurora Avenue. It features a fairly awesome array of aging neon signs, many that stay lit until morning. Your best bet is the Way West, a cloister of kitchenettes under the glow of impossible colors and drizzly clouds. Parts of the Way West have stood since 1938. In the intervening years, you could wash away the road dust in a diner and tavern. For a while, they called this spot the Bobilink, named after owners, Bob and Irene Lincoln. Grab a room and you'll walk a few steps into a hidden garden of well-tended greenery and rooms that reveal themselves like secrets in plain view. Turning the key, you'll enjoy the timewarp, flashing on Fonzie's apartment in *Happy Days*. There are wood-paneled walls, brown shag carpet, and a Magic Chef stove ("with uniburners!").

Head north toward Lynnwood, where pretty much everything at the Court of Monte Cristo Motel sags, from the concrete that tumbles down toward Highway 99 to the blue painted banisters that seem to have buckled under the weight of years. But the motel is friendly and the owners are determined to make this business work. The Cristo's owners — an elderly Japanese couple — have held out since 1984 but business has slowed since the terror attacks of 9/11. They hope with a genuine mixture of patriotic fervor and economic need that tourists will return to their quizzically named home. Photographers still seek out the quirky sign with its image of the Count. But give the rooms a try, too.

Out on U.S. 2, head east toward Leavenworth, a Bavarian-themed city where every dwelling is a haus and every hill is alive with the sound of music. Naturally, you'll want to stop at the Alpen Inn Motel. But also drop by the Timberline Motel with its stone cottages — each individually named for local trees like juniper, fir, and cypress. Even this far east of Seattle, Washington reminds you that this state is the espresso capital of the world with its many roadside coffee stands and "chalets."

On the other border, where Spokane still keeps the fires of the 1974 World Expo

WASHINGTON

warm, check out the Pine Lodge Motel. Driving onto the crumbly parking lot, you'll notice plastic sheets covering the windows and, perhaps, the Beatles crooning from a tape recorder through an open door. A fellow works on his bike while two rough looking dogs stand guard. Nearby, a pigeon coasts down to the pockmarked pavement, catching a free drink from the rainwater filled-potholes. You'll want to stay across the street at the Boulevard Motel, even though the trains roll along the hill just overhead. The Boulevard features all the standard amenities of a roadside rest stop, even a pool. Most notably, the motel features cheerful blue awnings and white clapboard siding. The Korean-American owners clearly take pride in their motel, but manage to throw in a bit of whimsy with a small collection of 1940s and 1950s-era roadside humor postcards for sale.

WEST VIRGINIA

When selecting a motel for the night, its name provides an important clue for what lies ahead. A motel's name offers a hint into the mindset of the owner, a taste of local history, a promise of temporary fantasy. The problem is that so many motels draw from a shallow reservoir of references: Capri, Holiday, Moonlight, Sandman, Sunset, Trail's End, Western, and other equally overused monikers. **West Virginia**, however, responds to this concern with some of the most unique names you'll find on the highway. These offbeat names include Count Gilu in Welch, Cow Shed in Pineville, Koolwink in Romney, Honey in the Rock in Beckley, and the historically challenged Forty-Eight States in St. Albans. Even more important than the names are the people who choose to maintain small motels in the Mountain State, a place not known for its tourist appeal.

Of course, the beauty of West Virginia — and its plentiful opportunities for climbing, hiking, and fishing — deserves more than a cursory glance. One friendly place to drop your keys, toss your bags, and settle for a while resides in the southern town of Hinton. For more than forty years, the Coast to Coast Motel, a Hinton landmark, has allowed part-time anglers to park their cars and cast their lines into the nearby river.

Along Highway 40 just prior to the Pennsylvania border, you'll encounter an entirely different vibe at the Valley Motel. Knock on the office door and be prepared to visit for a while with Judy. She'll be the first to tell you she is tired. She's tired of the late hours and she's tired of the endless cleaning. Once a road-tripper, traveling the country in an RV, she stopped in small towns to wash dishes when the money got tight, settle her accounts, and head for the horizon. Now, she tends to the wash and chow for part-time laborers who stay in her motel, rearranges the photos of her five children and thirteen grandchildren, and plans her next move: maybe a tiny house with a garden one day, just for her bird, dog, and cats. In the meantime, she confounds the depressed economy with the secret to successful motel management: "morning quickies, afternoon delights, evening prices."

In Wheeling, the Grove Terrace Motel maintains a somewhat more dignified presence along the otherwise dingy environs of the National Road as it makes its crossing through the state. Vince proudly shows a visitor the rooms that have remained unchanged since 1965 when his father built the place. The wallpaper still looks like the cover of a Victorian romance novel. The lime green shag carpet has been beaten down over the years. The abstract mosaic bathroom tile has withstood thousands of scrubbings. Looking down the road, Vince speaks with near reverence for the motels that lost the struggle: "I drive down the National Road and I see the old, nice motels I used to see when I was little and I miss them. But, you know, changing times, like horse and buggy. You accept it."

OAKWOOD MOTOR COURT
PRINCETON, W. VA.

WISCONSIN

A hand-tinted postcard from the late teens or early twenties depicts a free tourist camp in Baraboo, **Wisconsin**. Chugging automobiles navigate a dirt road past a motley cavalcade of tents and cottages. On the lower left-hand side, a fancy gent with a jaunty cap swings around from a bench, peering into the viewer of the scene. Nearby, one of the posted signs sports a fat black arrow inviting folks to drive in. Long replaced by parking lots, fast food joints, and more profitable businesses, this kind of free auto court recalls when local boosters and "progressive" chamber of commerce-

types imagined the money and goodwill to be earned by free municipal courts throughout Wisconsin and across the country.

Today, you'll have a difficult time finding remnants of these old courts. But there remains plenty to do in the Badger State. And, of course, most tourists are practically compelled by gravity to spend a night or two in Wisconsin Dells: land of fake volca-

noes, improbably beached fishing boats, pirate coves, bungee jumping towers, upside down buildings, haunted houses, water slides — and a small army of third-tier entertainment personalities who still manage to attract autograph-book waving fans. Naturally when you gather enough cars and enough people, you'd better maintain enough motels. Here, Wisconsin Dells delivers. While older local tourist courts like the Pine Dell Trav-O-Tel featured humble cabins that advertised indoor plumbing as a major selling point, contemporary motel complexes compete with sen-

sory-overload combinations of game rooms, play areas, and eye-catching signs.

Driving the strip through Wisconsin Dells, you easily spot the coolest motel of the bunch: the Flamingo Motel and Suites. In the play area, kids cavort under a giant mushroom that spouts a waterfall from its cap. Nearby they slide down an oversized green toad. And, of course, you'll struggle to find a more unique motel sign than a giant three-dimensional pink flamingo. Not too far down the road, the Holiday Motel responds with its classic doo-wop neon burst of red and yellow and, for good measure, a human-sized Statue of Liberty painted red, white, and blue. Wherever you stay in Wisconsin Dells, remember that the town was built for summer crowds and prices its accommodations accordingly. Don't show up in search of a cheap room without plenty of planning.

Or, just keep heading northwest toward Eau Claire in search of a quieter night's stay. Both the Eau Claire Motel and the Maple Manor Motel feature stunningly red neon signs that glow for miles, but the Maple Manor offers the extra touch of theme rooms that include a celebration of Viking and Packer Mania, as well as Parlors and Porches. Best of all, wake up the next morning to one of the nicest cafes you're likely to find on the road. The portions are huge and the prices are scandalously reasonable. Fill up on hot coffee and stare down the road. The cost of gas rises and the hassles of interstate travel continue to grow, but there's always a nice motel to be found when the sun finally sets.

WYOMING

A famed stop along the Lincoln Highway in Cheyenne, **Wyoming**, the aptly named Lincoln Court Motel reflects decades of mutating roadside nomenclature and design. Built in 1927, the motel began as a tourist camp built on land purchased by Pete Smith to grow potatoes. Figuring that more profit could be made from travelers than taters, Smith offered a reasonably

priced set of accommodations for folks willing to grab some sheets and towels and set up their own rooms. Postcards and guidebooks celebrated the then-named Lincoln Camp's most essential amenity: hot and cold running water as well as the

first in-ground pool in the state of Wyoming. Since those days, the family — three generations worth — added rooms, experimented with kitchenettes and private garages, and even endured the Court's nefarious "pink stage" (inspired by a trip to Las Vegas). Today, the Pepto Bismol color lies hidden under years of paint jobs and the Lincoln Court continues to grow.

If you find yourself heading north along Interstate 25 (sometimes you just can't help it), stop by the West Winds Motel in Wheatland. Built in 1963, the motel has weathered blizzards and bad times but has found fortune in the new owners who have taken on this project with the gusto of true believers. They've even added a park out front and attracted the notice of local boosters. "We kind of started a little chain reaction around here . . . got a few commendations from the city for helping the looks of the place."

Or, head north toward Douglas, home of the famed Jackalope — the mythical half rabbit-half antelope — and you'll think you've dropped onto the set of an old-time western when you pass the Plains Motel with its fake facade designed to evoke a rustic railroad town. Look around for a bit and you'll find Wanda who tells the story of her mother who bought the cabin camp in the 1920s when it only offered a set of

TEN SLEEP INN
TEN SLEEP, WYOMING

plain rooms with wood stoves and buckets. For two bucks a night, guests enjoyed use of a wrought iron bed with spring mattress and access to a community shower. Describing her railroad motif, Wanda explains that real railroad towns were hardly any more authentic, just a series of false fronts built with wood from local trees, hiding rooms that were little more than tents. Railroad builders would move the whole contraption down the line as they built the tracks. Now, with its stone sign and generations of guests, the Plains Motel offers an authentic roadside delight sure to last.

However you visit Wyoming, don't leave without a trip to Lusk, the town that recently gained fame in a series of adds by Microsoft touting its hometown appeal. As you'd imagine, the company moved on to newer focus groups but Lusk remains a quintessential western town, dependable for a rowdy rodeo and decent grub. Searching for a place to hang your newly purchased ten-gallon hat? You'd better stop right there, pard'ner, at the Covered Wagon Motel. Wired, friendly, and even boasting an indoor pool, the Covered Wagon is the nicest motel you'll find in these parts.

10 BLOCKS FROM DOWNTOWN CHEYENNE

Lincoln Court
WYOMING'S LARGEST AND FINEST
West U. S. 30 - - CHEYENNE, WYOMING

MEMBER OF AMERICAN MOTOR HOTEL ASSOCIATION

CREDITS

Alabama Beverly Motel – Jenny Wood • St. Francis Motor Hotel – Azalea City Printers Browns • Motor Court – Courtesy of Curt Teich Postcard Archives • Crescent Motel – Doyne Advertising. **Alaska** McKinley Park Hotel – H.S. Crocker Co., Inc. • See Alaska Decal – Farwest Litho Printing Co. • North Pole Alaska – House of Santa Claus. **Arizona** Hi There, Chum – Reg Manning • Sky Riders Hotel – Petley Studios • Starlight Motel – Jenny Wood. **Arkansas** Parkway Court – Courtesy of Curt Teich Postcard Archives • Arkansas, A National Opportunity – Authors' Collection • Bil-Roy Hotel – MWM. **California** Harold's Motel – Authors' Collection • Motel Inn – Crown Match Company • Route 66 Motel – Jenny Wood. **Colorado** Columbine Cottages – Courtesy of Curt Teich Postcard Archives • Chief Motel – Jenny Wood. Colorado Decal – Authors' Collection • Mountain View Courts – Courtesy of Curt Teich Postcard Archives. **Connecticut** A Victorian Village – Jenny Wood • Home Acres Motor Court – Kaeser & Blair, Inc. • Hartford Motel – Courtesy of Curt Teich Postcard Archives. **Delaware** Motel West – Jenny Wood • Pleasant Hill Motel – Tichnor Bros. Inc. • Delaware Decal – Authors' Collection • Park Plaza Motel – Mellinger Studios. **Florida** Sandman Motel – Jenny Wood • Driftwood Motor Lodge – The H & W Drew Co. • Tropical Palms Court – Tichnor Bros., Inc. **Georgia** Perry Court – Courtesy of Curt Teich Postcard Archives • Southern Motor Court – Henry H. Ahrens • Talbotton Motel – Jenny Wood. **Hawaii** Waikikian – H.S. Crocker Co., Inc. • Crouching Lion – Christian's LTD. • Hawaii Decal – Baxter Lane Co. **Idaho** El Rancho Motel – Jenny Wood • Flamingo Motel – Authors' Collection • Idaho

Potatoes – Authors' Collection • Rainbow Cottage Camp – Authors' Collection. **Illinois** Tourists – Andy Wood • O'Hare Inn – Courtesy of Curt Teich Postcard Archives • Murrie's Motel – Modern Advertising Co. • Illinois Decal – Authors' Collection. **Indiana** Covered Wagon Lodge – Tichnor Bros., Inc. • Complete Accommodations – Easy Aces, Inc. • Indiana Decal – Flex-Cote • Pine Haven Motel – Jenny Wood. **Iowa** Skylit Motel – Courtesy of Curt Teich Postcard Archives • Iowa Decal – Authors' Collection • Corey Motel – Jenny Wood • Cedar Lawn Motel – Midwest Sec., Inc. **Kansas** Log Cabin Motel – Jenny Wood • These Signs Go Together – James B. Clow and Sons • Thru Kansas Decal – Authors' Collection • Shangri-La Motel – Courtesy of Curt Teich Postcard Archives. **Kentucky** Wigwam Photo – Jenny Wood • Wigwam Village Decal – Authors' Collection • Kentucky Decal – Authors' Collection • Sander's Court – Colourpicture. **Louisiana** Sugar Bowl Courts – Jenny Wood • Alamo Plaza – Alamo Plaza Hotel Courts • Alto Tourist court – Fred R. Mackhart, Adv. Spec. **Maine** Turnpike Motel – Jenny Wood • Holiday Motel – Aladdin Business Service • Maine Vacationland Decal – Authors' Collection • Maine Idyll – Maine Idyll Motor Court. **Maryland** Alamo Court – Jenny Wood • Star Motel – Colourpicture • Nassau Motel – Nassau Motel • Maryland Decal – Authors' Collection. **Massachusetts** Best Camps – Best Camps Litho • Red Fox Motel – Jenny Wood • Arrow Gift Shop and Cabins – Tichnor Bros. • Massachusetts Decal – Authors' Collection. **Michigan** Elms Motel – Courtesy of Curt Teich Postcard Archives • Vacationland Decal – Authors' Collection • Rainbow Motel – MWM Co. •

Cadet Motor Courts – Jenny Wood. **Minnesota** Northernaire Motel – Jenny Wood • Minnesota Decal – Authors' Collection • New Ulm Motel – Thier Advertising Co. • Tourist Camp – Authors' Collection. **Mississippi** Jones Motel – E.C. Kropp Co. • Hitching Post Motor Inn – Jenny Wood • Alamo Plaza – Universal Match Corp. **Missouri** Little King's Hotel Court – Courtesy of Curt Teich Postcard Archives • Motel Key Lanyard – W.W. Wilcox Manuf. Co. • Munger Moss – Jenny Wood. **Montana** Derrick Motel – Authors' Collection • Chief Motel – Jenny Wood • Montana Decal – Authors' Collection • Bonander's Cottage Court – E.B. Thomas. **Nebraska** Rest-A-While Motel – Authors' Collection • Western Motel – Jenny Wood • Nebraska Decal – Authors' Collection • Campbell Court – Colourpicture. **Nevada** Lariat Motel – Jenny Wood • Scott Shady Court – Seabury & Co. • Nevada Decal – Authors' Collection. **New Hampshire** Mirror Lake Motel – Jenny Wood • Sleepy Hollow Motel – Herbert O. Thwing, Advertising • Tourist Village Court – Courtesy of Curt Teich Postcard Archives. **New Jersey** Moon Motel – Jenny Wood • Starlux – Starlux Motel • Lollipop Motel – Jenny Wood. **New Mexico** Blue Swallow Motel – Jenny Wood • De Anza Motor Lodge (Color) – Ventura Photo Associates • De Anza Motor Lodge (B&W) – Associate Service • Thunderbird Lodge – Match Corp. of America. **New York** 3 Star Motel – Jenny Wood • New York Decal – Authors' Collection • Circle Motel – Ad-View Post Cards • Your Home Away From Home – The Gladdon Co. **North Carolina** Mayberry Motor Inn – Mayberry Motor Inn • Log Cabin Motor Court – Log Cabin Motor Court • Pink Motel – Jenny Wood. **North Dakota** Sunset Motel – Jenny Wood • North Dakota Decal – Authors' Collection • Approved Motel – Appreciated Adv. • West Plains Motel – The Hafstrom Co. **Ohio** Victory Motor Court – Beals • Σ Baker's Motel – Courtesy of Curt Teich Postcard Archives • Old Orchard Motel – Jenny Wood. **Oklahoma** Desert Hills Motel – Jenny Wood • Oklahoma State Fair Decal – Authors' Collection • Sooner State Motor Kourt – Shedd Brown Mfg. Co. • Willshire Motel – Dexter Press, Inc. **Oregon** The Palms Motor Hotel – Jenny Wood • Elliot's Motel – Colourpicture • Come to Oregon Decal – Authors' Collection • Motel Oregon – Courtesy of Curt Teich Postcard Archives. **Pennsylvania** El Mor Motel – Mellinger Studios • Hood's Tavern and Tourist Court – Tichnor Bros. • Come to Pennsylvania Decal – Authors' Collection • Blue Ridge Motel – Jenny Wood. **Rhode Island** Blue Star Motor Inn – Jenny Wood • Motel Room – Simmons Company • Colony Motel – Author's Collection • Rhode Island Decal – Authors' Collection. **South Carolina** South of the Border – Jenny Wood • South Carolina Decal – Authors' Collection • Grand Motel – Aurora Postcard Company. **South Dakota** Kuilman's Motel – Courtesy of Curt Teich Postcard Archives • North Maine Motel – Tichnor Bros. • All Star Traveler's Inn – Jenny Wood with permission from the artist, Peter Teekamp. **Tennessee** Vacation Motor Hotel – Jenny Wood • Leahy's Tourist Court – Courtesy of Curt Teich Postcard Archives • Café Loveless – Authors' Collection • Tennessee Decal – Authors' Collection. **Texas** Helena Court – Seawall Specialty Co. • 66 Courts – Jenny Wood • Rambler Motel – Universal Match Co. **Utah** City Creek Inn – Jenny Wood • Utah Decal – Authors' Collection • Utah Motor Park – Courtesy of Curt Teich Postcard Archives • Lynada Motel – Colourpicture. **Vermont** Maple Center Motel – Forwards' Color Productions • Injunjoe Court – Injunjoe Court • Vermont Decal – Authors' Collection. **Virginia** Robert E. Lee Motel – Jenny Wood • Virginia Decal – Authors' Collection • Spring Court Motel – MWM. **Washington** Silver Moon Motel – MWM • Pine Lodge Motel – Jenny Wood • Washington Decal – Authors' Collection. **West Virginia.** Ring Bell – Jenny Wood • West Virginia Decal – Authors' Collection • Oak Wood Motor Court – Courtesy of Curt Teich Postcard Archives. **Wisconsin** Tourist Camp – E.C. Kropp Co. • Wisconsin Decal – Authors' Collection • Pine Dell Trav-O-Tel – Courtesy of Curt Teich Postcard Archives • Flamingo Motel – Jenny Wood. **Wyoming** Covered Wagon Motel – Jenny Wood • Ten Sleep Inn – J.L. Robbins Co. • Lincoln Court – Courtesy of Curt Teich Postcard Archives.

Andrew and Jenny Wood

Andrew Wood (Ph.D., 1998, Ohio University) teaches in the Communication Studies department at San Jose State University and wrote *Road Trip America: A State-by-State Tour Guide to Offbeat Destinations* (Collectors Press). He also co-authored a book about computer-mediated communication and co-edited a book about reality television. Jenny Wood (B.A., 1994, Berry College) has been a photographer since 1986 when she began work on her AA degree in Fine Arts. Her photographs have been featured in an art show, theaters, advertisements, two album covers, and in USA Today. This is their first book collaboration.